GRASS ROOTS PASTORS

Grass Roots Pastors

A Handbook for Career Lay Ministers

Leonard Doohan

1817

Harper & Row, Publishers, San Francisco

New York, Cambridge, Philadelphia, St. Louis
London, Singapore, Sydney, Tokyo

GRASS ROOTS PASTORS.Copyright © 1989 by Leonard Doohan. All rights reserved. Printed in the United States of America. No part of this book may be used or reproduced in any manner whatsoever without written permission except in the case of brief quotations embodied in critical articles and reviews. For information address Harper & Row, Publishers, Inc., 10 East 53rd Street, New York, NY 10022. Published simultaneously in Canada by Fitzhenry & Whiteside, Limited, Toronto.

Library of Congress Cataloging-in-Publication Data

Schaef, Anne Wilson.
    Escape from intimacy.

    1. Relationship addiction.   2. Love—Psychological
aspects.   3. Intimacy (Psychology)   I. Title.
RC552.R44S33   1989   158'.2   88-45698
ISBN 0-06-254860-3

89 90 91 92 93 MCN 10 9 8 7 6 5 4 3 2 1

To Bev and Lolo and family

Kia Tukulolo Beverley Moe Famili.
Hounga 'Ae Kaumea Hange Pe Ha Famili
Ofa Atu.

ACKNOWLEDGMENTS

I thank Fr. Philip Murnion for permission to use ideas from his article "Eight Ways To Improve Parish Participation," published in *Today's Parish,* March 1983, pp. 19–21. I also thank the editors of *Today's Parish,* copyrighted 1983 by Twenty-Third Publications, Mystic, CT 06355.

Several years ago I was invited to participate in group discussions of the Center for Post-Conciliar Spirituality in Rocca di Papa. Ideas in chapter 2 on group development and in chapter 3 on planning resulted from those discussions, and I am grateful to the participants. I particularly acknowledge my indebtedness to Juan Bautista Cappellaro and his colleagues. While I know of no English publication of their work, I refer readers to *Presenza: Quaderni di Spiritualità,* vol. 5, 1972.

I wish to thank those friends and colleagues who read the initial draft of this book. Their suggestions were valuable in rethinking sections of the text. I thank Ms. Karla Huffine for her expert assistance in preparing the manuscript.

My special thanks to my wife, Helen, and our daughter, Eve-Anne, who are always major contributors to my work, in their understanding, support, and love.

CONTENTS

PREFACE

Baptismal commitment is the most important and wonderful focus of our religious lives, and in our generation it offers possibilities of satisfying experiences, personal and communal fulfillment, and excitement in our day to day activities in the name of the Lord. Being a Christian, and particularly a Catholic, is thrilling as we deal with our splendid task of proclaiming Jesus in new ways for changed times. Those who love both the Church and life struggle to bring them together in the hearts and lives of contemporaries. The Christian body, which is principally laity, tries to discern what needs to be said today and finds that in these years the perennial values of Jesus' Good News are proclaimed in new ways. Many laity today read the gospel and find it challenges them to be involved in Jesus' work in a new way, and any sincere discernment of this trend must conclude that it rings with truth. Once again the world of our past and the world of our future both focus on the centrality of Jesus whom laity wish to proclaim in new and relevant ways. The future can frighten, but it can also excite, and laity do not need to look at it as a dangerous enemy but as a vocation that draws us to the Lord.

The Church is at a turning point regarding ministry, when, sadly, the number of clergy and religious are decreasing with no foreseeable hopes of increasing. And many of today's outstanding pastors are no longer priests but laity. Some would call our present experience a crisis of choice for the Church. Christians, especially the laity, must respond, motivated by the future and not by the past. Always on the frontiers of life, the Church, like any organization, first experiences growth at the edges, not in the center structures. Laity are at the edges, and among ever-increasing numbers there is a sense of joy and enthusiasm as they increasingly breathe new life into our Church.

More competent than ever before, laity are both picking up the ministries left by decreased numbers of clergy and religious and creating new ministries to respond to real human need. Filled with faith, a deep spirit of sacrifice, respect for each individual's dedication, and an extensive love of the Church, they minister with courage, aware that a better future is not the fruit of a dream but of the hard evangelical task of changing lives—one's own, and others'.

We are called to realize ourselves as Church in the future, to develop new possibilities of living out the message of Jesus in our rapidly changing world. Reading the Scriptures, laity see the ever-present call to ministry but see that it has a new focus, calling themselves to be instruments of the Lord, coworkers in a splendid task.

I see no likelihood that the future direction and vision of the Church will filter down to the people from somewhere high up in the structure, rather, it will percolate up from the grass roots dedication and experience of laity. We continue to love our brothers in hierarchical ministries, but the effective leadership of many seems severely weakened. An organization can be short on personnel, funding, and education and still do something, but when short on the right kind of leadership there is not much anyone can do.

In the past many valid ideas were stifled at great loss, and even in recent years we have seen international leaders showing increasing distrust of some local bishops, theologians, priests, women, and faithful in general who have been identified as deviants from established positions. This faithless approach to the faithful is at times linked with the rather primitive notion that people are changed by authorities. Some Church authorities at times portray an addictive attachment to historical forms of authority, power and money, and their own selective criticism of sin (sexual immorality is criticized, financial immorality is covered up), their own interpretations of teachings, their selective appreciation of tradition, their unwillingness to eliminate sexism, their circular use of Canon Law (Canon Law forbids it so it can't be done, but in some cases Canon Law already says it can't be done so it won't be done), their encouragement of ultraconservative "bounty hunters" for those who dissent. In fact, the 1985 Extraordinary Synod criticized a selective reading of Church values (1985 Extraordinary Synod, The Final Report, *Origins* 15 (1985), I, 4). One of today's paradoxes is that our Church is becoming unified and fragmented at the same time.

International leadership is impoverished, and partly as a consequence religious indifference is a very real choice for many. Fortunately new lay leadership is emerging to complement the outstanding leadership of post-Council years given by some clergy and religious. Laity in ever-increasing numbers are committing themselves to lay ministry. This refocusing of ministry will bring substantial changes in the Church, more than the changes resulting from Vatican II. At the time of the Council, many had no motivation for change, whereas now we are faced with a critical choice if ministry is to be maintained. Many of the components of Christianity are subject to change as they decline in relevance and call forth new interpretations. The task of accepting the challenge to change can be done with optimism. As we ask whether certain facets of the Church are valid anymore, we will need to accept pluralism with love and make effort toward a shared vision. Catholic pluralism never imposes uniformity in nonessentials but allows enriching diversity, while always striving for unity. However, the extremes—right and left, which are both pessimistic—become less and less forms of Catholicism and need to acknowledge they are no longer in union with the main body of the Church.

While some, disenchanted with the present, look to the past and despair of Christ's relevance to contemporary society, many laity, dedicated to ministry and aware of their equality in baptism, are giving the Church new life, as they have so frequently done in history. Rooted in the local Church, they are finding new, significant, nonclerical priorities for the Church.

Much of the present theology is not representative of lay experience, but through quality lay leadership we see a self-determination and self-direction of laity in spirituality, worship, ethics, and professional life. This demands candor and truthfulness. We have done a lot of talking since Vatican II. Now a new kind of talking is needed that will produce a theology that has pastoral validity and will lead to the recovery of the mature roles of laity in our Church. This is the work of community discernment, a common listening to the Spirit who knows what future is best for us. This revitalized consensus of the faithful, applied to ministry, is also coming from the rich experiences of lay ministers. Provided we do not become fundamentalists to our own experiences, rigidly using our own experiences as criteria to measure others' different circumstances, then some of these responses of career lay ministers are illuminative when critically expanded in light of faith. Ministerial responses are rarely if ever global; they are local, as each person tries to faithfully live out the call to serve. As a result, rich experiences of ministry involvement at the local level are contributing to a new understanding of a vital, relevant, pluralistic Church.

Lay ministers with pastoral skills that enrich the Church provide much of the leadership in the recovery of the dignity of laity. This book focuses on those lay pastoral ministers, and their gift of life and love to the Church.

I have chosen a series of interrelated topics that are critically important for laity who work in ministry today. Chapter one, "Lay Ministry Yesterday and Today," deals with the history of ministry from New Testament times to today. It shows the consistent involvement of laity in Church ministry and indicates the negative side effects of some historical developments in clerical and religious life on the laity. Thus, laity working in ministry can insert their own vocational development within history, rather than seeing it as a twentieth century development due to decrease in numbers of clergy. The growing numbers of laity working in ministry with clergy and religious leads to the second chapter, "Collaboration." The Vatican Council's ecclesiology of communion, reinforced by the 1985 Extraordinary Synod, is visibly portrayed in collaborative ministry. For today's lay ministers, collaboration is the contemporary way of living as Church, and this chapter deals with the ecclesiological vision of collaboration. Chapter three takes this vision a step further by considering the practical implications of collaboration, and the efforts needed to make it successful. These efforts form the contemporary spirituality for career ministers. Of the many forms of lay ministry, this book focuses on those that are within Church structures. Chapter four deals with the obstacles and opportunities that laity face when their ministry is within the institutional Church. Not all ministry implies leadership, but increasing numbers of career lay ministers find themselves in the roles of pastoral leaders, and chapter five stresses the need to develop the vision and skills of appropriately Christian forms of leadership. Chapter six acknowledges that laity in ministry face many tensions which can be experienced as oppressive or creative. The final chapter identifies these tensions and suggests ways of dealing with them. Thus, all the chapters—history, ecclesiology, spirituality, mission, leadership, and effectiveness—are closely connected. Together they reveal and support the growth taking place at the grass roots where new lay pastoral leaders are enriching the Church.

I divide each chapter into three parts: theological reflection, critical issues, and topics for reflection and discussion. I hope that the combination of theology, practical issues, and reflection will lead to an integration of important issues facing the minister today: the nature of ministry itself; the various expressions of ministry including collaboration with lay, religious, and clergy coworkers; the realities of working as a minister within Church structures, providing pastoral care, and surviving the tensions in ministry.

I have talked with many lay ministers individually and in groups. I have also discussed ministry issues with intervocational staffs and teams. I have distributed questionnaires to a wide variety of dioceses and individual lay ecclesial ministers. This book offers material for study, discussion, and personal integration, together with suggestions regarding some of the many practical problems met in the new lay ministries of recent years.

A fresh kind of approach to Church is appearing among dedicated lay ministers who pastor in our Churches in increasing numbers. Simple, generous, evangelical; competent, skilled, visionary; encouraging and enthusiastic, these dedicated career pastoral ministers are a special blessing to this generation. This book is a small sign of my earnest wish to be supportive of this life of ministry.

GRASS ROOTS PASTORS

Chapter 1

LAY MINISTRY
YESTERDAY AND TODAY

L̲ay Ministers Speak on Ministry

Reflections

Introduction
Biblical Perspectives on Ministry
The History of Ministry before Vatican II
Vatican II and the Universal Call to Ministry
Theology of Ministry
Interpretational Guidelines for Christian Ministry
A Subjective, Personalist Approach to Ministry

Critical Issues in Contemporary Ministry

Refocusing Church Ministry
Rights of Laity in Ministry
Contemporary Ministries
Defining Ministry

Topics for Reflection and Discussion

Your Ministry: A Personal Reflection
Questions for Group Sharing

Some Career Lay Ministers' Concerns about Lay Ministry

Selected Reading

Lay Ministers Speak on Ministry

At the beginning and end of each chapter I have placed a series of direct quotes from career lay ministers concerning the subject matter of the chapters. These comments were gathered from career lay ministers around the United States who participated in a survey I distributed. From the several hundred who wrote to me, I have selected quotes that express the feelings of many. I see their dedicated ministry as a source for reflection on the future direction of ministry in the Church. Their positive comments at the beginning of each chapter show their vision, dedication, and spirituality. Their concerns at the end of each chapter challenge the Church to appreciate these ministers' struggles and to correct institutional obstacles to their growth. While the whole book is the fruit of working with lay ministers, these introductory and concluding comments of the ministers express their feelings in their own words.

After thirteen years in ministry people respond to me proudly.

•

I've always felt for the poor. That's what Jesus told his disciples: to love people and serve the poor.

•

My ministry enhances the quality of my life by giving my life deep meaning and deep satisfaction, and by bringing to my life wonderful people and good friends.

•

I love my ministry. I feel it's where God wants me to be.

•

The motivation for my ministry is my indebtedness to my God, response to his call, and my own personal sanctification.

•

I see new models of ministry emerging: communities of priests, religious brothers and sisters, and lay men and women, ministering as a unit to God's people.

•

The qualifications for ministry are simply that one believes this is where God wants you. The work is sharing with others your own life story so that others can find God within themselves and their brothers and sisters in Christ.

•

Life, prayer, suffering, and more prayer prepared me for the present demands of my ministry. I say prayer because here my heart and soul have been torn open to receive others with the love of Christ. Having the heart of God is crucial for what I do. Discernment too is critical as well as a source of energy and love that goes far beyond myself.

•

I would encourage others to dedicate themselves to lay ministry. There is a vast field open and there are feelings of satisfaction to be had. Also there is the knowledge that you are doing this for God.

Reflections

Introduction

Dedicated lay men and women have given hope and vitality to every generation of the Church, from Aquila and his wife Priscilla in New Testament times to the many Jean Vaniers, Rosemary Haughtons, Donna Hansons, and Dolores Leckeys of today. Following the many lay evangelists of the first decades of Christianity, there were lay teachers and prophets who inspired, educated, and organized the faithful. Before the clerical Church authorities organized the hermits and monks of the desert, there were laity who created these lifestyles and gave new direction to dedication to the Lord. Before there were religious orders, there were visionary laity whose charisms, and spiritual maturity had developed these styles of life. Often individual laity like Catherine of Siena or the dukes of Europe called the Church to reform. Spiritual movements in our own century may now be mainline Church activities, but they started with the personal ministry of laity like Frank Duff, Chiara Lubich, and others.

The lay-centered Church has benefited enormously from the ministry of untold numbers of laity, some of whom focused their ministry in outreach to heal and transform a broken world, and others of whom directed their ministry to enrich the internal life of their Church. History shows beyond question that the Church constantly needs both forms of lay ministry. In every generation since Jesus, laity have ministered to the needy, challenged injustices, transformed their families, brought a Christian vision to social and political life, educated the ignorant, and focused progress. They also were coworkers of the apostles. They protected the hierarchy from unorthodox teachings of Arianism; organized, financed, and even created forms of monasticism, mendicant and active religious orders; participated in Church councils; advised popes and bishops; and enriched theology. Some gave life to the spiritual movements and many others maintain living Churches today.

To worry about the "clericalization" of laity today, or to refer to those laity who minister to the internal life of the Church as "paraclericals," shows a lack of appreciation of both history and theology. Lay ministry has always had two foci—service to the world and service to the Church.

Prior to Vatican II the Catholic structures of ministry had ceased to mirror the universality of New Testament ministry, and lay ministry was not valued as it ought to have been. Ecclesiastical power and control were frequently seen in the failure or refusal to relinquish ministries that others could perform.

The Holy Spirit has blessed our own generation with a worldwide renewal launched by Pope John XXIII. The Second Vatican Council which he called focused on the understanding of the Church as the community of the People of God, it affirmed the universal call to holiness, and set the stage for a major effort to upgrade the image of all the baptized. In the eighties, efforts to restore the legitimate place of laity in the Church's life and mission have centered particularly on the recovery of the authentic nature of ministry. Church renewal has increasingly become a renewal of our understanding of ministry.

There have been few attempts to institutionalize the reforms of Vatican II in new ecclesiastical structures, but the few marginally successful attempts have been in new approaches to ministry—team, intervocational, or lay—and in the new developments fostered by apostolic movements. Moreover the contemporary crisis in ministry could not be solved by increasing the number of clergy. Although provoked by a decrease in full-time ministers, the current crisis calls for a new approach to ministry. Vatican II valued lay contributions to ministry as they have been throughout history, and the Council called the whole Church to appreciate the gifts of laity. Conversion to this conviction places us on the road that inevitably leads to a new understanding of Church.

When we speak of ministry we can refer to an equality in ministry that is rooted in the sources of our faith. The equality does not exclude differences in ministry, nor that some are more directly related to the mission of the Church than others. Equality does not lead to a leveling to the lowest common denominator, since the baptized, rejoicing in their own gifts, can rejoice that others are better in preaching, scholarship, or social service. Equality does not mean democracy. Some are in the community to organize it, some to lead it, and others to occupy roles judged insignificant by the world's so-called wise.

In seeking to recover an appreciation of our equality in ministry we seem at times to be comparing apples and oranges. Radical equality presumes equal opportunity for formation, study, skill development, prayer, and evaluation; it presumes equal commitment of financial resources. Where these are lacking there is no actual equality even though there ought to be. Certainly the status quo portrays inequality, but we must ask ourselves if the current inequality portrays faithfully or unfaithfully the original commission of Jesus Christ and if it manifests a commitment to capitalize on the ministry of all.

Biblical Perspectives on Ministry

Ministry is so much a part of Jesus' life that it is inseparable from who he is. He ministers to all, whether Jews or Gentiles, teaching, preaching, and healing. He lives ministry, urges it on some, and commands it at times. He calls people from all walks of life to follow him and imitate his suffering servanthood. There is the fisherman Peter, Mary of Magdala, Nicodemus a member of the Sanhedrin, Joanna the courtier, Matthew the tax collector, Mary the mother of James, Judas the businessman, Martha and Mary from Bethany, Nathaniel the skeptic, Simon the patriot, Salome who later anointed him for burial, the wealthy Joseph of Arimathea, an unnamed rich young man, blind Bartimaeus, and many unnamed men and women from Galilee. Jesus calls these followers, instructs them, guides them in their own ministry, and takes some of them with him to see and experience his ministry first hand. He singles out twelve of these to represent the twelve patriarchs and to symbolize the definitive, or eschatological nature of his followers.

Jesus picked his disciples from the laity, with the exception of Nicodemus. In general he rejected the Sadducees and Pharisees, and in their place called forth a new chosen people to minister to the world. Jesus does not give details of his understanding of the nature of ministry, nor does he give a list of appropriate ministries. He gave no structure or order to ministry, nor did he establish any specific offices beyond the general designations of disciple, apostle, and the Twelve. In fact our present terms office, ministries, hierarchy, priesthood, and diaconate have no immediate counterparts in Jesus' mission. There are no references to a ministerial priesthood, no suggestion of a structured approach that gives authority in ministry to an elitist inner group, and no distinctions between a passive laity and an authority-bearing clergy. In fact, the important offices of contemporary Catholicism—pope, bishop, priest—are not referred to at all in the New Testament in the way they are understood today.

Jesus laid the foundations for a community of disciples and instituted his Church as the new Israel. However, the forms and structures of ministry do not come from Jesus but from the early Church. Moreover, as the early Church struggled to institutionalize the challenge of Jesus, they felt no obligation to specific forms of ministry or structure. Rather we find a variety of church orders and ministries. James governed his province with a college of elders. Matthew's church is led by prophets and teachers. Paul retains a personal authority even when traveling away from the churches he founded, and his letters are never addressed to individual church leaders. John's communities seem to be led at first by charismatics and later by chief elders—a development that led to polarization as we see in John's third letter. Thus, neither Jesus nor the apostles see any structures or offices as permanent or needing to be the same for everyone.

In early New Testament times, all faithful shared in decision making, mission priorities, and ministry. They also chose from among their community those who were to exercise group leadership. Moreover, local communities differed in their approach to ministry and their choice of structures for ministry. Gradually presbyteral church order replaced the fluid order of early times. Already the later letters—pastorals, Peter, and James—presume an institutionalizing of ministry and a primacy of presbyteral order. Charismatic leadership has gone, the general faithful are dispossessed of their shared authority, and organized ministry takes on structures Jesus had deliberately rejected. This ecclesiasticalization and sacerdotalization of ministry is viewed by some as divinely guided, while others consider this divorce from roots as a perversion of New Testament ministry. Whatever value is to be given to the historical and political developments in the organization of ministry, Jesus' original challenge was equally to all without distinctions. Jesus called others with a conviction that commission, charisms, leadership, presence, sacramental influence, and possibility of success were for all. To the question, Did Jesus entrust his mission to a hierarchy or to the universal Church? the answer can only be the latter.

The History of Ministry Before Vatican II

The generation following the apostles still retained a variety of ministries and structures of ministry. There were presbyters, charismatic individuals, elders, deacons, deaconesses, widows, prophets, and teachers, each of whom exercised a primacy in administration dependent upon the structure chosen by the local community. Moreover, the chosen leader celebrated the Eucharist without any thought of priesthood. Early Christian writings speak of teachers and prophets presiding at the Eucharist *(Didache),* or other eminent individuals with the consent of the people (Clement), or those who confessed their faith under persecution (Hippolytus). The person who presided at the Eucharist was not "ordained" for this service.

Gradually two forms of ministry developed: institutionalized officers chosen by the people—the overseers and presbyters—and a spontaneous form of ministry exercised by Spirit-filled charismatics—the prophets and teachers. At first the latter were more important, but gradually presbyterial church order was established throughout the universal Church, and while this was collegial at first, we soon see strong monarchical bishops emerging like Clement of Rome, Ignatius of Antioch, and Polycarp of Smyrna. By the beginning of the second century, the community's collegial exercise of ministry yielded to the central authority of an overseer who was also celebrant of the Eucharist. Models of ministry such as we find in the Acts and in Pauline Letters disappear, and the stage is set for the ecclesiasticalization and resacerdotalization of Christian ministry along the lines of the Jewish priestly aristocracy with their Sanhedrin and high priest.

The period of persecution increased the need for organization, education in faith, and centralized authority, and gradually all forms of ministry—catechetical, liturgical, and social—were absorbed by the overseer and his presbyters or deacons. During periods of persecution the dicotomy between a ministerial elite and a passive people is evident. This is intensified after Constantine's decision to make Christianity the religion of the empire. The notion of priesthood, up to this time reserved exclusively to Christ and the Christian community, is now applied to the celebrating minister, something the early Fathers had rejected. The exclusion of laity from ministry is then supported by doctrinal statements on the priesthood and on the rights to preach, teach, and govern, which were presumed to have been granted by Jesus exclusively to the apostles and their successors.

By the fourth and fifth centuries bishops dominate the life and ministry of the Church, ministry and office are identical, and a clerical monopoly of ministry is established that will last for fifteen hundred years. With peace in the empire, Christians increased in numbers and became passive toward ministry. Presbyters are sent by their bishops to preside over local churches, their power no longer coming from the choice of the people, but through ordination to the priesthood. Church leaders who previously gained their authority from the community now receive it from the sacrament that confers an indelible character on the recipient. Priests are no longer ministers who serve the people but ministers who serve the cult. They alone can effect the Eucharist. They are different—a difference symbolized in the law of abstinence and locally in the discipline of celibacy, practices that the New Testament nowhere linked to ministry.

Although Jesus' call to ministry was universal, the Church began to see itself as composed of two unequal parts: the priests who governed and ministered and the passive servant laity. The former must never be tainted by the latter. They thus live apart and are urged to avoid all contact with the wicked world (all Christian at this time) and especially with women. Priests are considered superior in all senses, and their ministry becomes increasingly a sanctuary ministry.

Throughout the Middle Ages, ministry, other than sanctuary ministry, was centered on the monastery, where it became less a service of outreach and more a dedication to prayer and asceticism. The monastic life became the ideal also for the clergy, and laity were downgraded even further.

Many outstanding developments took place in the Middle Ages, including periods of major commitment to reform, but all forms of ministry remained centralized in the clergy. Ministry became increasingly a private matter of the priest or monk and was viewed in the context of orders and especially the Eucharist, not in the context of ecclesiology—a pathetic situation that continued until Vatican II.

The lack of authentic ministries of education, prayer, and liturgical growth were contributing causes of the Reformation. In fact, ministry was exclusively priestly and reduced to a magical understanding of the sacraments over which the priest alone had power. The reformers insisted on the priesthood of all the baptized, challenged the clergy caste by removing the discipline of celibacy, questioned the sacramental "character" of priesthood, and began the disintegration of hierarchical control of society. Papal responses in Trent reaffirmed traditional understandings of ministry without offering any new synthesis or new structures of ministry.

Since the Reformation all ministry has been strictly controlled by the hierarchy, and while laity could be involved in apostolic service individually or as groups, such ministry could never be called "Catholic" or be seen as official Church service. The ministry of 99.5 percent of Catholics was unofficial and not the ministry of the Catholic Church! The former practice of institutionalizing lay activities by turning the dedicated individuals into religious gave way to ecclesiastical control of Catholic Action. The presumption throughout was that Jesus' mission and ministry were entrusted exclusively to the hierarchy, a position that claimed the support of tradition— tradition that more honestly should be seen as the often repeated position of the Roman Church.

Catholic and official ministry were reserved exclusively for clergy, many of whom were ordained absolutely without a community to minister to, a situation that had been solemnly condemned by the early Church. Priestly monopoly was maintained, laity were disenfranchised, Catholicism was characterized by a pervading passivity, ministry was reduced to a cafeterialike distribution of spiritual goods, and the priest became an institutional mechanic called to keep the spiritual machine running smoothly.

The history of ministry before Vatican II is both the history of dedicated clerical service and of lost opportunities, and it is difficult to say which is greatest.

Vatican II and the Universal Call to Ministry

Vatican II further consolidated the power of the bishop and of Rome, but also forcefully presented theological foundations for a universal calling to ministry. The Council's vision of the Church as the People of God, primacy of baptism as the sign of dedication, universal distribution of charismatic gifts, priesthood of all the baptized, focus on the local church, and acknowledgment of laity's specific role in Church ministry, contributed to a new approach to ecclesial ministry.

The Council documents referred to laity as living instruments of the Church (Dogmatic Constitution on the Church 33:2) who have an indispensable role in the mission of the Church (Decree on the Apostolate of the Laity 1:1), a ministry that is exclusive to them. They share in the priestly, prophetic, and royal functions of Jesus (Laity 2:2), receive charisms for the benefit of others (Laity 3:3), and are called to the same holiness as priests and religious (Church 41:1, 7). They cooperate in the Church's universal mission (Church 30:2, 33:1), and their ministry is so necessary that without it the priest's effectiveness will be limited (Laity 10:1). In fact, without the laity's collaborative ministry the universal Church remains stunted (Decree on the Church's Missionary Activity 21:1). Thus, laity are urged to contribute to the development of the life of the Church (Church 33:4), with their spirit of coresponsibility, (Church 33:3), inventiveness (Pastoral Constitution on the Church in the Modern World 43:4), and planning (Mission 36).

Lay ministry specifically includes evangelization, world development, charitable services, the fostering of family spirituality, and social involvement. Laity also have the right and duty to minister by participating in the liturgy, building up the community of the local church, and taking active roles in the coresponsible development of local parish life.

The Council focused the Church's ministry in new areas: family life, civic and international life, culture, education, liberty, and peace. All these are areas of Church ministry in which the experts are laity. This set the scene for extraordinary developments in which the laity emerged as ministerial specialists. The Council gave laity an awareness of their call to ministry, challenged priests and religious to realize they are incomplete without the ministry of laity, and called all to share, collaborate, and move forward together.

The Council led to a period of tension between the hierarchy and laity who had become aware of their call to ministry. We have seen parallel ministries develop: hierarchially controlled forms and spontaneous lay forms in which laity are willing to work in union with the mission of the Church but not be controlled. Laity involved in ministry full-time or part-time are now so numerous that we need to find new structures that will preserve both ecclesial unity and baptismal freedom.

The Council proclaimed the universal call to ministry based on baptism, not on mandate. While the hierarchy maintains good order in the ministering body of the Church, it does not grant the right to be involved in ministry, for that comes from the Spirit who endows the faithful with charisms for their task. In light of Vatican II, it is incorrect to refer to laity as "nonordained" since in baptism they receive the laying on of hands and anointing that sets them apart for ministry.

We have traveled full circle and returned to an understanding of the Church in which all have ministerial rights, sealed with the character of baptism, gifted with the Spirit, talented to serve, and responsible to themselves and their Church.

Theology of Ministry

Much of the spiritual renewal since the Vatican Council has focused on ministry. Many laity have dedicated themselves to parish, diocesan, or individual spontaneous ministries. Others, having joined spiritual movements, have found that all of them have a ministry component to their vision of Christian life. Laity understand ministry in different ways than before the Council, are convinced that everyone is called to service, anticipate a new direction in the Church's future ministries, and recognize that new approaches imply a serious questioning of the traditional clerical monopoly of ministry. It is also increasingly clear that ministry is a broader concept than church work, as it is also evident that some ecclesiastical professionals see their task as a job and not a ministry.

Increasing numbers of the faithful have a new perspective on ministry. If involved, they enjoy it and find it rewarding. For many it is an expression of their own identity. Two trends are identifiable: a growing awareness that service for others is a necessary part of baptismal dedication and a realization that in these years God is calling many men and women to make service for others a professional commitment. A spirit of service and a ministerial commitment are closely related but distinct. The former is part of the gift of faith, is in every mature Christian, and shows itself in concrete attitudes of selfless service when occasions present themselves at work, in one's family, in civic life, or in the Church community. This enthusiastic and selfless service for others is not a ministry but is part of the spirit of Christianity and a manifestation of the priesthood of all the baptized.

A ministerial commitment is something quite different, even though it grows out of the Christian spirit of service. This ministry has its source in the gift and challenge of Christian initiation, manifests itself in the proclamation of gospel values, is a professional commitment, is lived in ecclesial interdependence, and is ecclesially authenticated.

The source of ministry is Christian initiation, not ordination and not ecclesiastical mandate. Through baptism, confirmation, and a loving community, the Holy Spirit gives the faith, hope, and love that produce a ministerial vocation. As baptized followers of Jesus, successors to the original ministering communities, disciples have the rights and obligations of ministry. Their dedication is the prime ministerial reality in the Church. Their's need not be "church work," but it is unquestionably the work of the Church. Through these servants of grace, the power of the apostles becomes alive again. Some of these ministers will commit themselves to a particular ministry that they can enter through ordination or through a vowed life, but others will not. The source of ministry is found not in ordination or profession, since these are possible without ministry, and ministry is possible without them. Rather the source is Christian initiation.

The gift and challenge of ministry leads to a vocation of service that proclaims gospel values. Historically the Church often made mistaken choices for power and control, and sometimes its officials portrayed unhealthy, unspiritual, and nonministerial attitudes. Today we still find a tension between personal vocation and institutional commitment, but the particular institutionalized ministries are not the only ministries. Thus, the succession of apostolic ministry is found in the whole Church, not through mandate or delegation or participation in the hierarchy's ministry, but through the lived gospel values of untold numbers of faithful.

Faithful living of the servant challenges of the gospel requires knowledge of the Scriptures on which ministry is based, not only as a source of prayer and piety, but more as a source and resource for one's ministry. Understanding is not secondary, but since ministry portrays one's understanding of the Church, ministry is always educational. Ministry manifests what we claim to be, and the minister must be aware of the educational impact of his or her lifestyle.

Ecclesial ministry is a professional career commitment and can be full-time or part-time. Many part-time and volunteer services manifest more than the spirit of service that comes from baptism. The dedication is a serious professional and vocational commitment and fulfills all the requirements of authentic ministry. These part-time ministers contrast with others who, although working full-time for the Church, do not see their job as a ministry. Authentic ministry is not only a function but it includes the attitudes and vision of ecclesial union. Interdependently we build up the body of Christ.

A major characteristic of Christian ministry is that it is carried out in union with, and in the name of the Church. Ministers serve with an awareness of their interdependence with all other ministers. In fact, to live in union with the Church is the first component of all ministry. In the past, this union was made visible in the hierarchial structure of some ministries. The choices the Church made were not exclusive choices—there are others. In fact, even the formalized ministries of bishop, priest, and deacon developed slowly and manifested an ecclesiastical division of labor and a development of career specialists. Although these forms of ministry were not seen to be necessary in the early Church, they were soon established and eventually absorbed all other ministries. Nowadays these three are a small part of the ministerial vocation of the Church. They are important but still secondary; they serve the nonclerical ministers who form the prime priestly reality of the People of God.

A final characteristic of ministry is that it is ecclesially authenticated—that is, it is recognized by the Church as a contribution to the extension of the kingdom. Authentication implies evaluation, and it should be universally applied to all ministers whether lay, religious, or priestly. The authentication must be ecclesial but need not be ecclesiastical except to maintain good order. As we evaluate each other's ministry and authenticate its value to the Church—expressly or tacitly—we assist each other without regulating; we cooperate without thinking we delegate. Ministries do not exist because clergy share their power, they exist already and the officials of the Church simply recognize them without having the right to manage them, except to maintain good order. Part of this authentication should be allowing the development of new models of ministry that reflect ecclesial response to new needs.

Ecclesial authentication implies evaluation and accountability for one's ministry. These are ways in which everyone in the Church is dependent on others. There is nothing wrong with this. However, we have evolved to inappropriate and unacceptable dependencies on the one hand, and a total lack of accountability on the other. Both trends are seriously jeopardizing the possibility for genuine ecclesial authentication.

Interpretational Guidelines for Christian Ministry

Christian ministry, rooted in scripture, continually develops throughout history, at times taking on new forms. To be authentic, ministry must not only embody the unchanging values dealt with in the last section and be indirectly traceable to Jesus, but ministry must also be relevant to changing times. This section complements the last one and suggests five questions that can be used to judge the authenticity of Christian ministry, and its appropriateness for the eighties and nineties. True for all ministry, these questions are particularly suitable for judging contemporary ministries. In fact, they can show how some new ministries are authentic, whereas some traditional ministries have become inauthentic because they are irrelevant.

1. *Is the ministry relevant?* Does ministry satisfy real needs, or is it merely cosmetic ministry that makes people feel good but is not significant for their spiritual health? The Church's presence is one thing, but quality of presence is another. Does ministry respond to

the signs of the times and embody relevant ways of challenging people to live distinctively as Church in the eighties and nineties. Some forms of ministry tell us what needs were in times past, and we may need a reordering of our priorities in ministry for it to be relevant today.

Ordained ministries serve the inner life of the Church, but the major ministries of the Church serve the needs of the world. Are our ministries relevant, pastorally valid, and central to the gospel's impact on contemporary society? If not, then we are not the authentically ministering Church for today.

2. *Is ministry being facilitated or controlled?* The interrelationship between ecclesiology and ministry must be taken seriously. Ministers experience tension in their service, sometimes feeling that their ministries are not facilitated but controlled by others who have a different understanding of the Church. The ministry of authority seeks truth, shares love, and serves the common good by unifying, serving, and building up the community. Sometimes the impression is given that some Church officials fear losing the security that their acquired power has brought. Here manipulation enters the community, and officials can thwart ministry development rather than welcome it. Many lay ministers receive the impression that the universal radical equality in ministry is against the will of the management elite.

The ministerial life of the Church may be facilitated, authenticated, supported, and challenged. When controlled and restricted in order to maintain the power of an inner elite very serious questions of conscience arise. It will be sad if the increased involvement in ministry pursues a liberation movement to throw off unjustified and oppressive control. The faithful are interdependent in ministry, and major structures should never take upon themselves what can be done by substructures.

3. *Is ministry authentically discerned?* Since the source of ministry is the Holy Spirit in baptism, the Church must carefully discern the Spirit's focus for ministry in each successive generation. To move from an imposed uniformity in ministry to a deliberately willed solidarity requires discernment of spirits. Validity of ministry comes from the community, many of whom read the gospel in the same way today and conclude that new ministries are needed. Moreover, many new ministries are authenticated in others' experience of need. The

consensus of the faithful is perhaps the best single measure of ministerial relevance today. This is not to exclude obedience, but it does remind us that obedience is mutual, and authority in the community is never a substitute for discernment or knowledge. Each believer is responsible to discern the needs of this period in history and coresponsibly direct the Church to the ministries the world needs.

4. *Is ministry a reaching out from a loving Church?* God's covenant was made with the people, not their officials. We together are the ministering, convenanted people, and before we do anything we are called to be the loving community of God. Church officials are not among us to give permission, manage our ministries, and delegate their authority. The Spirit works in many ministering faithful; what they do is not as important as who they are as a result of their faithful acceptance of call. This personalist approach to ministry leads to mutual respect and a valuing of both institutionalized and charismatic ministries.

Part of this experience of a loving community is a sense of Church in each of us. Ministry may be local but vision is worldwide. In this context new ministers should also draw ordained ministers into ecclesial solidarity since the isolation of some institutional ministries leads to loneliness and a sense of rejection. We need to present ourselves above all as a loving, ministering community.

5. *Is ministry changing?* Some of the faithful are afraid of the future and cling to nonessentials of Church life and ministry. Ministers must observe changes in our society, be ready to change in order to satisfy new needs, and present perennial values in new ways. We know we should change, but we often stagnate rather than discover new ways to live ministry. Ordained ministries in particular seem sealed tight against any change. The silence and neutrality of some church officials is simply a loud and clear commitment to the status quo, and if death comes to some of our ministries, some officials will need to accept their own guilt by association.

The Church is a social organism and evolves like any other. It has changed, can change, and will change—even though slowly. Structures of ministry are provisional, and a reductionist understanding that limits acceptable structures to clergy leads to ineffectiveness and ultimately to inauthentic ministry. New forms of ministry are not threatening to the dedicated, updated, and active deacon, priest, or bishop but only to those who really do not know where they are going.

We must be open to change in models of ministry, models that may be different in different cultures. We need to give birth to new models that true leaders can find attractive, models that are collegial.

As we face crisis and changes in our Church and in our ministry, we can maintain our vision of equality in ministry by an ongoing evaluation that asks: Is the ministry relevant? Is it being facilitated or controlled? Is it authentically discerned? Is it a reaching out from a loving Church? Is it changing as times change?

A Subjective, Personalist Approach to Ministry

In any consideration of ministry a subjective and personalist approach must predominate over any objective emphasis. He or she who ministers is more important that what is done. There are no great ministries and no menial ones either. The major value is baptism that modifies a personality, making an individual a person of the Church.

I am unpersuaded by theologians and church managers who define laity by their secularity, "being in the world." This is an inadequate basis for vocational or ministerial distinctions. To suggest that priests and religious are not "in the world," or although in it live in a "formally" different way, is meaningless. To try to identify the specifics of 98 percent of an organization is a futile pursuit. Their characteristics are those of being members of the Church and no further specifics are possibly applicable to all 98 percent.

The structures of contemporary ministry are feudal. Although the role of the priest is changing, the specific ministry of the priest can only become clear once the radical equality in ministry has been established. This latter is the context and interpretative key for the former. Crisis in role clarification of priest and religious will remain until the ministry of the baptized is established. In all decisions regarding ministry, Church officials should exercise a preferential option for laity.

All ministries are equal because we all share the same cause of ministry—the Holy Spirit; we receive the same call and commissioning of Jesus; we receive a common ministerial vocation in baptism; we are endowed with charisms as the Holy Spirit sees fit; we are consecrated into the same common priesthood; we are equally endowed with the threefold office of Christ: priestly, prophetic, and kingly; we are fed as ministers with the same sacramental life; we authenticate our ministry in the consensus of the faithful.

In seeking to recover an appreciation of our equality in ministry, we reviewed historical developments from biblical times to the Second Vatican Council. Our history shows an essential equality and a secondary structuring as a result of political and ecclesiastical developments. The Vatican Council came full circle to reemphasize the universality of ministry.

We also saw the major components of ministry. Ministry has its source in Christian initiation, manifests itself through gospel values, is a professional dedication that can be full- or part-time, is lived in ecclesial interdependence, and is ecclesially authenticated.

Among the serious questions concerning ministry, we should ask not is it institutionalized, but is it relevant? not is it controlled, but is it facilitated? not is it in apostolic succession, but is it authentically discerned? not is it official, but does it come from a loving Church? not is it always the same, but is it changing with changing needs?

We must stop pretending that the only thing that can be done is what we have always done. So many of the faithful are enslaved to the recent past because they have not taken the time to study the development of Christianity. We can search for a new vision of pluralistic ministries that are authenticated without being institutionalized.

While equality in ministry is a vision, there are also practical things that can be done. It would be desirable to eliminate the words "lay," "clergy," and "minister," from our vocabulary, even though it may be difficult, if not impossible, to do so. We can name the forms that ministry is taking—and be surprised at the variety and richness. New ministers should remember the importance of visibility and accept it in public gatherings. We can encourage new ministers to stay in their profession by supporting new models of ministry with the aid of sound employment practices: job descriptions, job security, just salaries, advancement opportunities, and support structures. If already ecclesial ministers, we can be mentors for others who see professional ministry as a vocation. We can be assertive in our support of equality in ministry. In fact, for the current imbalance to continue all that is required is that good men and women do nothing. If equality in ministry is to be long-lived then it is crucial that new ministers give serious attention to religious education. For the many bishops, priests, and deacons who abandoned study long ago, their pastoral practice reflects a decline. New models of ministry must preserve the commitment to study, lest they become seeds that grow quickly but are scorched by the intensity of the sun. A refined sign of our conviction on the equality of ministry is our mutual prayer for each other's ministry, for wisdom for each other, and for the ability to create suitable environments where God can give grace. If we are to be dedicated to a vision of equality in ministry, then we must be courageous in the choices we make, in the principles we defend, in the willingness to reinterpret the ministerial vocation that Jesus offered us. As we work for equality in ministry we should prudently establish support systems where ministers can find life and refreshment from the burdens of ministry.

Jesus' gift of a call to ministry is available to all the baptized. Let's not smother it but rather nourish it in each other so that we can be apostolic leaders in our Church.

Critical Issues in Contemporary Ministry

Refocusing Church Ministry

The largest ministerial group in the Church today is the laity. In the past one's ecclesiology led to one's understanding of ministry, whereas now ministry is generating a new ecclesiology. Moreover, there are many people the Church does not know what to do with, but they know what to do with the Church, and they are dedicating themselves to ministry in such numbers that a refocusing of ministry is taking place.

The history of ministry includes developments that are responses to changes in the people's understanding of the nature of the Church. Contemporary Christians, influenced by the ecclesiological developments of Vatican II can ask themselves, What reforms in ministry are necessary as a response to this new vision of Church? However, the Church's ministry is not to itself but to the world, a world that shows its needs and hopes in the signs of the times. Thus, responsible Christians can also ask, To what services do the current signs of the times call the Church? As new forms of ministry arise in the Church, the faithful need to know which can be considered authentic and how they can gain authorization. The issue that arises regarding contemporary ministries is no different than that dealing with the earliest ones. Laity may well ask, Since

Jesus did not establish ministerial structures, how did early structures gain authorization, and how do contemporary ones achieve it? In any refocusing of Church ministry, laity will have a major role. In fact, historically the mission and ministry of the people was carried out by clergy and religious, and this challenges laity to ask, What ministries do we want clergy and religious to perform for us today?

This refocusing of ministry needs to start with the laity. Present attempts to clarify the role of priests and religious are destined to fail unless we first clarify the vocation and mission of laity. In fact, some models of priesthood become catchalls for roles that belong to others.

A useful contribution to the refocusing of Church ministry is for the faithful to identify their own understanding of priestly ministry. What is their model of priesthood? What do they value most in the priest? Does their family benefit more or less from priestly ministry than they did five years ago? What are the priest's most important services: spiritual leadership, sacramental and liturgical presiding, social action, or something else? In answering these and similar questions, laity can identify possible changes in their image of the priest, and how Church ministry is evolving—other ministers now doing what the priest used to do, others' ministries now being valued more than some of the priest's, some of the priest's valued ministries not needing ordination.

This refocusing of Church ministry, our contemporary search for authentic ministry, is part of a self-evaluation of our fidelity to the call of Jesus. We cannot stagnate but must discover new ways to live ministry. History shows that the structures of ministry were originally provisional. Our knowledge about the origins of ministry challenge us to constantly evaluate our current focus.

We critically analyze contemporary ministry to root it in New Testament practice and vision. Changing the outward forms of ministry is a serious undertaking and should only be done as a way of being faithful to Jesus. However, at times, an unwillingness to change can leave previously important ministries as irrelevant cosmetic ministries that foster the soothing services of a comfortable religion. In a future shock world of rapid change, Christians need to refocus ministry and implement change rapidly to avoid irrelevance. In fact, we may need to face the profound contemporary changes with tentative solutions in experimental ministries.

Rights of Laity in Ministry

The history of ministry is so unusual, often manifesting a put-down of lay life. Each stage in history presupposes an ecclesiology. Some views of Church presumed to have existed, or claimed to be ideal, are seen by many laity as quaint and unrealistic, and, were they ever to be extensively imposed, they would be viewed as repulsive. Some of our current structures and practices are not conducive to lay ministry and need to be changed. Oppressive ecclesiastical regimes whether international, national, diocesan, or parochial lead to discouragement and reduce people to inactivity. People who feel bad about the institution spend time thinking and worrying about it. Their outreach in ministry decreases, and the Church becomes progressively useless to the world it is meant to save. The Church must have a structure that shows trust in the people.

Career lay ministers have many rights, recognized in the New Code of Canon Law. In times of discussion on the extent of lay involvement in ministry, career lay ministers do well to know their rights. As an aid in this self-education and justification of ministry, a list of the appropriate Canons and their teaching is given.

Canon Law establishes the following rights for all the faithful:

- Canon 204: To participate in the threefold office of Christ, and to share in the mission of the Church.
- Canon 208: To equality and dignity, and to cooperate in building up the Body of Christ.
- Canon 211: To evangelize.
- Canon 212: To express needs and desires to the pastor, to advise him, and to express organized public opinion.
- Canon 213: To receive the spiritual benefits of the Church, especially Word and sacraments.
- Canon 214: To follow one's own spirituality.
- Canons 215, 298, 299, 321–29: To association, to found and to organize groups for ministry purposes.
- Canon 216: To promote apostolic undertakings.
- Canon 217: To Christian education.
- Canon 218: To academic freedom.
- Canon 219: To freedom in one's choice of a state in life.
- Canon 220: To protection of good name, and to privacy.
- Canon 221: To just process in Church courts.

The following canons establish specific rights for laity:

- Canon 225: To participate in evangelization individually and corporately.
- Canon 226: To educate their children.
- Canon 227: To all civic freedoms of other citizens.
- Canon 228: To assume some ecclesiastical offices and to participate in decision making.
- Canon 229: To Christian education and research and to receive authorization to teach theology.
- Canon 230: To installation in the liturgical ministries of acolyte and lector, in the temporary ministries of lector, commentator, cantor, and when necessary to proclaim the Word, preside at liturgical prayers, administer baptism, and be eucharistic ministers.
- Canon 231: To a living wage if permanently hired.

Among the code's unprecedented list of rights and privileges of laity are the following:

- Canon 519: To cooperate with the pastor in fulfilling his mission.
- Canon 759, 766: To be called upon to preach when necessary or useful.
- Canon 776: To assist the pastor in cathechetical ministry.
- Canon 784: To be sent as missionaries.
- Canon 785: To be catechists in the missions.
- Canon 861: To be deputed to baptize.
- Canon 910: To be a eucharistic minister.
- Canon 943: To be delegated as extraordinary ministers for exposition of the Blessed Sacrament.
- Canon 1112: To be delegated as official witnesses to preside at marriages.
- Canon 1248: To celebrate the liturgy of the Word when there is no Mass.

The code upgrades the roles of laity in their local parish life.

- Canon 517 permits the bishop to establish a team of laity under the supervision of a priest.
- Canon 519 reminds pastors to cooperate with laity and use their assistance.

- Canon 529 states the pastor's obligation to promote laity in their mission.
- Canon 536 points out that the parish council gives the pastor help in fostering pastoral activity.
- Canon 537 speaks of the laity's aid to the pastor in the finance council.

In certain circumstances the code also allows laity to exercise diocesan offices.

- Canon 483: Chancellor and notary
- Canon 492: Member of diocesan finance council
- Canon 494: Business manager of the diocese
- Canon 1421: Judge
- Canon 1435: Promoter of justice or defender of the bond
- Canon 1483: Procurator or Advocate

Contemporary Ministries

Christian communities throughout the world are either allowing or seeking the development of a rich variety of lay ministries. Historically the origin, power, and authentication of ministry resided in the community, and the hierarchical control of ministry, which only climaxed in 1917 when Rome claimed the exclusive right to choose bishops, is an aberration of the faithful's basic rights. Now we are again seeing the spontaneous development of ministries from the communities' visions of a Church in service to the world and from the communities' own needs.

These ministries are often organized on the local level, gain their vitality and direction from parish leadership, and are frequently catalogued on computer so the staff can call on them as needed. Where ministry is assigned on the basis of sex, women frequently are pushed out by men especially from authoritative positions, but the women's ministry behind the scenes remains a major contribution, frequently being leadership whereas men have often limited themselves to management. There is a great variety of approaches to regional ministries, dependent on the local church and regional problems, local structures, and cultural differences. These ecclesial ministries manifest the focused dedication of laity. In addition to the ministries established by Canon Law, we see ministries of internal service to the local church.

A sign of our times is the establishing of paid professionals in ministry in our local churches. Some of these receive payment directly from the local church while others receive income from those they minister to in a freelance ministry. As the churches rapidly accepted the Director of Religious Education (DRE), others are enriching their church with the specialization of other ecclesial ministries such as:

- Pastoral associate, assisting the pastor in the varied responsibilities of ministry
- Director of religious education with specialization for children, young adults, and adults
- Youth ministers with their enthusiasm, skills, and cultural sensitivities
- Pastoral minister for the elderly or sick
- Retreat and prayer formation personnel associated with parishes, retreat centers, or spiritual movements
- Traveling lay evangelists who feel called to preach renewal programs
- Laity who work full-time for national or international spiritual movements
- Men and women who exercise a regional, national, or international ministry of music, gospel proclamation, or consulting services
- Parish council members who give time, expertise, and prayer to organize, budget, and administer the parish's overall pastoral plan
- Spiritual growth committees who develop prayer groups, faith-sharing groups, retreats, and parish renewal programs
- Volunteers in educational ministries for children and adults
- Eucharistic ministers who have broadened their ministry to serving the sick, shut-ins, and lonely
- Local church counselors for youth, families, marriage, and unemployment counseling
- Music ministries that help the congregation prepare and celebrate worship
- Organized ministries of parish social service to peace, justice, and human rights
- Sanctuary movements and other challenges to unjust decisions of government

- Ministries of hospitality to newcomers, the sick, and the abandoned
- Specific sensitivity to those who suffer from job related frustration—the unemployed, those suffering from burnout or under-challenge including religious and clergy
- Ministry to the divorced
- Visiting and financial support of the sick and poor
- Community services to enrich the quality of parish life though socials, meals, and entertainment
- Increased awareness of the responsibility for educational and formational ministry associated with parenting and godparenting

People today are more concerned than they used to be with ministering to our needy world. The true focus of all Church ministry is service to the world. Laity have developed a commitment to better our world, have become aware of a new sense of sin, have increased the communitarian dimension of spirituality, and have accepted responsibility for global changes. There is a spirit of discovery in many laity's approach to ministry. Many take a genuine ministry approach to the following areas of need:

- Ministries of family life
- Removal of sexual discrimination and challenges to civic and ecclesiastical harassment of women
- Faith-filled observers of modern culture with a view to integrating faith and culture
- A dedication to excellence in one's profession, in technological development, and research
- Political service as a form of building Christian values into community
- Educational, artistic, and cultural enrichment
- Striving for world peace
- Right-to-life movement

Some of the contemporary emphasis on ministry has resulted from the decreased numbers of clergy. Saddened by the losses, laity are also taking hold of the opportunity to increase awareness of their own call to ministry, realizing that while ministerial priesthood is essentially different from the priesthood of all the baptized, it is not greater than it. Laity, ministering often as a married couples, are arriving at clear conclusions regarding the presumed necessity of celibacy for major ministry, finding that it has no relationship to increased availability.

Defining Ministry

Since one's approach to ministry results from one's ecclesiology, there are several ways of describing ministry. I have already distinguished between the general spirit of available service, which is part of everyone's baptismal responsibilities, and a ministerial commitment. It is the latter alone that concerns us here. It may be worth asking whether we need to define ministry, or do we just live as we think we ought to live and leave the synthesizing or theologizing to others. Some will undoubtedly choose to explore, but model descriptions can clarify, direct, and focus dedication. The following definitions complement the section on theology of ministry.

Ministry as Ecclesiastical Office.

History and Canon Law acknowledge many services performed by the faithful who have a spirit of ministry, but specific established ministries correspond to ecclesiastical offices and require ordination.

However, some holders of ecclesiastical office are not involved in real ministries, or do not live their office as a ministry. "Minister" is as often a misnomer for clergy as it is for laity. Some Church officials do not have their ministry authenticated by the people, who go to others for the ministry they need. While holding an ecclesiastical office, they are not involved in genuine ministry. The diaconate, priesthood, and episcopacy developed slowly, partly as a response to political pressures, and only later were legitimized. Rather than limit ministry to ecclesiastical office, we should first acknowledge that laity and clergy together are the ministerial force of the Church.

Ministry as Pastoral Care.

It has been traditional to focus ministry on the bishops or pastors and speak of them as proclaimers of the Word, celebrants of the liturgy, spiritual leaders of the believers, educators of the parish, and governors of the community. However, this ideal is rarely attained by one person. Moreover, many pastors are no longer teachers, forced as they are to become pastoral technicians to assure good celebrations. If, as often happens with this model, you emphasize the minister as coordinator or enabler, the model becomes dissatisfying to many who believe they have individual leadership qualities. When management is emphasized, this is often what you get and all you get. The exclusive approach to ministry as pastoral care is turning many clergy into circuit riders.

Ministry as the Acceptance of an Established Function.

When the concept ministry is described with an awareness of both law and the broader vision of Vatican II, it is possible to suggest the components of ministry in the eighties. Ministry implies designation for the performance of a recognizable function on a regular basis (at least semipermanent). The function is recognized and authorized by the believing community and exercised in its name. Motivated by Christian instincts, the minister attempts to convey gospel values. (See James A. Coriden, "The Contours of Ministry in the Eighties," *Social Thought* [Fall 1980]: 3–9.) However, authorization by the community is frequently reduced to hierarchial mandate. Some of today's most powerful ministries have never received designation or authorization. Moreover, ministries are increasingly situational and not permanent, and some of the most dedicated and professional ministers work in volunteer ministries.

Ministry as a Vocation.

Most people who involve themselves in ministry do so because they feel called by God, are convinced they are qualified to respond, and are sent in Christ's name to faithful who need them. However, this approach needs discernment, since many who feel individually called find their ministry is not authenticated by the faithful. Vocational commitment has frequently lacked updating in skills, evaluating of performance, and refocusing to ecclesial need. This model raises some serious questions: How is competence and effectiveness to be evaluated, and to whom is the minister to be accountable? How can the community discern whether the personal or ecclesiastical vocation is authentic?

Ministry as a Career Commitment.

This approach views ministry as the dedication of those who have undergone training, claim special knowledge and skills, are paid for their services, and administer a specialized aspect of the local church's stable and habitual needs. However, some professionals may not have the knowledge and skills but only claim to have them. This understanding of ministry can produce conflict when the hired minister is not as qualified as volunteers. Many qualified professionals lack the maturity of experience and need support from parishioners in their early years. Moreover, conflict arises between what one is trained to do and what needs doing right now.

Ministry as Church Service to the World.

Since the Church is the sacrament of God's love for the world, its primary mission is to minister to the world. This basic priestly, prophetic, and servant mission is carried out principally by laity. In this view what laity do is unquestionably ministry, but what clergy do is probably better described in some other way, possibly as administration, overseeing, or community service. However, it is very difficult to change the use of vocabulary and it has been traditional to use "minister" for inner-church directed functions. This model of ministry is too broad. When everything is ministry, then nothing is. We need new concepts to describe the common service of all the baptized.

Ministry as Relationship.

Establishing and nurturing relationships is particularly important for career lay ministers. They need to maintain a healthy self-concept and enthusiastically preserve their own lay identity. Since a community is frequently unwilling to give a new lay minister the immediate acceptance it gives a cleric or religious, career lay ministers must foster deep relationships with the people they serve in order to establish their own credibility. However, this relational view must also be complemented with responsibility for education in faith and prophetical challenge of the community.

Ministry as the Evangelizing Work of the Church.

The nature of ministry is formed by six characteristics. (See Thomas F. O'Meara, *Theology of Ministry* [New York: Paulist Press, 1983], 130). Ministry is doing something; for the advent of the kingdom; in public; on behalf of a Christian community; which is a gift received in faith, baptism, and ordination; and which is an activity with its own limits and identity. However, some ministries can be accomplished outside of the Christian community and only tacitly approved. This understanding can by useful provided what is done on behalf of the kingdom is interpreted broadly.

The above models highlight valuable components of a ministerial commitment. Their views complement the components of ministry indicated in the reflection section of this chapter.

Topics for Reflection and Discussion

Your Ministry: A Personal Reflection

1. Describe what ministry means to you.

2. Specify the sources of your ministry.

3. List the five most important components of ministry.

4. What were the objectives of your ministry five years ago?

5. How has your ministry been refocused in recent years?

6. What personal Christian rights and privileges do you feel are threatened in your ministry?

7. Identify the new directions you expect ministry to take in the next ten years.

Questions for Group Sharing

1. What are the essential components of Christian ministry?
2. List the ten main religious needs you hope to have satisfied by the Church. How many are satisfied by a clerical minister?
3. When did the bishop attain the power he has today? Who gave it to him? When did the community stop electing its own bishops? When did Rome claim the right to nominate all bishops?
4. To whom should the priest or bishop be accountable? What role should the faithful play in evaluating their ministers?
5. Do you experience lay ministry to be effective?
6. List the concrete procedures that you think the local parish or diocese should establish in order to give some security to laity who dedicate themselves to career ministry.
7. Can the same ministries be equally suitable in any of the world's cultures?
8. Is the work of every bishop and priest a ministry?
9. Does your local church faithfully live the social teachings of the Church in regard to the laity, religious, and priests who minister to it?
10. What are the excuses you or your acquaintances use for not accepting and facilitating lay ministry?

Some Career Lay Ministers' Concerns about Ministry

Our pastor is very supportive, but some parishioners are not.

•

Most people encourage my ministry. In fact, only priests do not. Those priests with whom I work are verbally quite negative.

•

In ministry I have received a mixed response from clergy and laity, including a lack of cooperation from some clergy, sex discrimination from both clergy and laity, and particularly a lack of understanding and suspicion from clergy and laity about the lay vocation—"why don't you enter the convent?"

•

Being Christian means ministering. To the extent we don't, to this extent we've not understood or we have failed in our commitment to Christ and the Church.

•

I find that an all male, hierarchical structure that glorifies celibacy inhibits the development of lay ministry.

•

I'm underchallenged.

•

Older views of Church seem to inhibit the development of lay ministry. These people simply prefer the way it used to be.

•

There is often lack of trust, lack of communication, desire for power, jealousy, lack of accountability, and personal empire building.

Selected Reading

Anderson, James, and Ezra Earl Jones. *Ministry of the Laity.* San Francisco: Harper & Row, 1986.

Fisher, Douglas, ed. *Why We Serve: Personal Stories of Catholic Lay Ministers.* New York: Paulist Press, 1984.

Kinast, Robert L. *Caring for Society: A Theological Interpretation of Lay Ministry.* Chicago: The Thomas More Press, 1985.

O'Meara, Thomas F. *Theology of Ministry.* New York: Paulist Press, 1983.
Pittenger, Norman. *The Ministry of All Christians: A Theology of Lay Ministry.* Wilton, CT: Morehouse-Barlow Co., Inc., 1983.
Schillebeeckx, Edward. *The Church with a Human Face: A New and Expanded Theology of Ministry.* New York: Crossroad, 1985.

Additional Reading

Doohan, Leonard. *The Laity: A Bibliography.* Wilmington, DE: Michael Glazier, Inc., 1987. See sections 16, 21, 22, 24, 26, 28.

Chapter 2

COLLABORATION

L̲ay Ministers Speak on Collaboration

Reflections

Introduction
What Is Collaboration?
Collaboration and Images of the Church
Laity and Collaboration
Spiritual Value of Collaboration
Facilitating Collaboration
Treating Others as Partners
Initiating Collaboration

Critical Issues in Collaboration

Forming Collaborative Groups
Models of Collaboration
Working in a Noncollaborative Structure

Topics for Reflection and Discussion

Personal Questions on Collaboration
Questions for Group Sharing

Some Concerns about Collaboration Expressed by Lay Ministers

Selected Reading

Lay Ministers Speak on Collaboration

I am the only nonordained member of the pastoral team here (and therefore the only female as well), but despite this there has always been equality, collaboration, and strong support on this staff.

•

In a good collaborative experience you know that what you are doing is supported by all. When you feel discouraged, having people to listen to you, encourage you, and understand what you are going through is great! You don't feel alone, and ideas are spread by many instead of one person.

•

Communication skills enhance our willingness to work together as a team of equals. Power and control must be shared.

•

There's more creativity when we collaborate, responsibility becomes coresponsibility, work is divided up so that no one gets a messiah complex. The ideal is when a team is multivocational, then it images in some way the real local church. Finally, risks are easier to take when you feel supported.

Reflections

Introduction

We have reflected on the historical development of ministry and the current need to refocus ministry. Perhaps the most important aspect of the refocusing is the emphasis on collaborative ministry. "Collaboration" means working together, but post–Vatican II developments show that the Church often concentrates exclusively on the sociological aspects of structural changes rather than on the spirituality that underlies them. Thus the Council's teaching on collegiality has not led to a renewal of structures and the use of authority because it has been seen merely as a form of checks and balances rather than a way of spiritual life for those who exercise authority. Thus, the issue of collaboration among clergy, religious, and laity must be put in the context of faith and seen as a new vision of shared ministry. As increasing numbers of laity work with other vocations, it is crucial that we capitalize on this occasion to stress the implied ecclesiological vision and the underlying spirituality.

We live in a world that values collaboration, and modern people have grown to expect it at home, at work, and in social and civic life. Excellent and innovative contemporary businesses and political groups foster collaboration at all levels of their organizations. In all walks of life we witness the end of efficacy in hierarchical structures and a dedicated search and discovery of collaborative forms of organization. A Church that is less than our human ideal will face major problems in its evangelizing work.

An increasing gap between hierarchy and laity has been evident for at least two decades. Collaboration encouraged by the Council quickly gathered dust, and while there is still a lot of talk, there is also considerable indifference and understandable opposition to collaborative forms of administration and ministry. In the context of negative developments in the numbers of Church personnel, collaboration is like asking a powerful politician to train the seemingly incompetent person who has just ousted him. In addition to individual reluctance to collaborate, there continues an unwillingness to confront the reality of accelerated change and new needs and a complacent belief that things will work out, vocations will increase, and this terrible period will soon be over. Many Church personnel are willing to sacrifice their status and vocational privileges, but they lack both the vision and the skills to initiate collaboration with their lay colleagues, for in many cases priests and religious were not trained to live in a lay-centered Church.

Catholicism's recent history evidences considerable resistance to collaboration. Some Church personnel in positions of power are unwilling to collaborate because they wish to retain power and maintain control over vision, future development, and financial resources. Thus we now have many failed organizations and much loss of institutionalized vision resulting from a lack of authentic delegation and sharing. Some prefer to dry up and die rather than see others take up their vision and mission.

The Church needs to dedicate itself to collaboration and to take leadership in doing so rather than be seen as merely reacting to pressures. The 1985 Extraordinary Synod stressed the ecclesiology of communion as the central idea of the Council and saw collaboration as a concrete expression of this vision (1985 Extraordinary Synod, The Final Report, II, C, 1 and 6). Both fidelity to the Council and an adequate portrayal of a new image of Church require collaboration. Moreover, without collaboration the Church will encounter great difficulty in bringing Christ's call to modern men and women. Nowadays the effectiveness of our ministry depends on communion manifested through collaboration.

What is Collaboration?

Collaboration is not a way of doing something more efficiently, but a way of being Church more authentically. It is a result of baptism, confirmation, and faith in the Spirit's charisms in us all. Rooted in our understanding of the Church as a communion of the People of God in which each member shares in a universal call to holiness, mission, and ministry, collaboration is a communal expression of the priestly, prophetic, and servant responsibilities of all the baptized.

Collaboration requires the friendship of faith, where love and mutual respect show in a conviction that we are moving to a common vision and would be incomplete without each other. Collaboration is a faith- and love-filled response to others that leads to hope. An essential element in Christian life and ministry, collaboration is a sign of equality in faith. It requires in each baptized person love and humility, interior freedom, selflessness, a desire to seek truth and serve the common good, and conviction that all are gifted to contribute to the ecclesial ministry we share. It fosters harmony in plurality, diversity, and dissent, and encourages attentiveness to the Spirit in others, reciprocal openness, and sensitivity to new forms of God's call. Collaboration is a Christian form of shared responsibility and essentially a form of ongoing discernment.

Although collaboration is a practical expression of ecclesial communion and shared responsibility, it is a sacramental witness to our union in baptism. It presupposes an appropriate vision of the Church and an appreciation of the community aspects of Christian life and call. It requires peace of soul, freedom of spirit, prayer, and discernment. It implies availability to others in love, a readiness to dialogue, an acceptance of discerned truth, and courageous fidelity to build the ecclesial community together.

However, collaboration is also a practical expression of faith in which believers actively and willingly take responsibility and initiative in a common ministry. It is more than advice or consultation and leads to full participation in decision making in keeping with the equal status in baptism that all Christians possess. It is a genuinely Christian form of shared authority that seeks truth, shares love, and serves the common good.

Christian collaboration is not possible between unequal parties, between those who are the organization and those who belong to the organization or associate with it. As an expression of Christian faith collaboration is a sign of equality, mutuality, and reciprocal openness. This is true even when dealing with the special charisms of individual groups within the Church, since charisms are more important for their ecclesial commonality than they are for their distinctiveness. Differences will always exist among the faithful as signs of richness and vitality. Christian collaboration affirms the distinctive qualities of individuals and groups and can preserve them for the common good by unifying, serving, and building up the community.

Collaboration relates essentially to the Church's common witness of its faith. Irrespective of whether the team is made up of priests, religious, or laity, it is preferable to speak about Christians collaborating in a specific ministry. The principal focus being Christian highlights the essential value of the contributions of all and presupposes that training, understanding, and participation may be highly developed in any of those collaborating in the specific ministry. We seem to live comfortably with the fallacy that priests and religious can train and educate laity, even in the specifics of laity's distinctive charisms and ministries, while the laity are understood to be without this ability. Yet most dimensions of the Church's ministry today are maintained principally by laity. Just as many priests and religious are unwilling to collaborate, so too with laity, large numbers of whom are closed to all forms of collaboration. However, the largest body of dedicated Christians today are laity, and they certainly number more than all priests and religious combined. In fact, they are the major ministerial group in the Church.

Collaboration and Images of the Church

If nothing significant could happen in the Church without the clergy, then we would have a clerical Church. However, the Church is a community of disciples with equal dignity and rights before it is a hierarchical structure. The Council's ecclesiology of communion, reinforced by the Extraordinary Synod in 1985, is visibly portrayed in ministry through collaboration. The Extraordinary Synod draws the conclusion that there must therefore be participation and coresponsibility at all levels of the Church's life (1985 Extraordinary Synod, The Final Report, II, C, 6). This is precisely the image of the Church we find in the New Testament. Thus, while we may be passing away from a period of privileged positions, careerism, and ministerial control that resulted from social, political, and educational restrictions of past ages, we are not moving to something new by emphasizing collaboration but returning to styles of baptismal responsibility grounded in New Testament times. Our baptismal coresponsibility, lived through hierarchical structures in more recent centuries, is again lived through collaboration as in the early days of the Church.

The real foundation for ministry is baptism and confirmation, not priestly ordination or religious profession. In past centuries, lack of education and religious awareness prevented a responsible living of baptismal dedication through collaborative ministry, but this is no longer the case. Lay participation in all dimensions of Church life now contributes to the molding of a contemporary image of the Church. This implies daily struggle since collaboration is lived in local groups that are different, polarized, and only partially identified with one another. Collaboration is not only a way of ministering together but a way of being Church.

Generally we want an image and structure of the Church we can cope with. In fact, images are frequently used as means of control, and people give descriptions of the Church that keep them in power. Current models of the Church call for communion of life and collaboration in ministry. They imply willing cooperation, new styles of collaboration, a collegial spirit, and an appreciation of unity at the local level, even in the smallest basic ecclesial communities. The Synod proceeds to speak about "diverse partial realizations" of collegiality, the appreciation of "the principle of subsidiarity in use in human society," and "collaboration . . . on the regional, national and international levels" (1985 Extraordinary Synod, The Final Report, II, C, 6).

People can work together in ministry, cooperate in planning, and pray or discern call without sharing the same understanding of

Church. However, Christian collaboration implies the striving for common goals, common vision, and common ideals of life. Christian collaboration, besides being a working together in ministry, is a common dedication to build a shared vision of Church. It is both a capitalizing on pluralism and a striving for unity at the same time.

Laity and Collaboration

Apostolic coresponsibility of laity results from baptism. They have an active part to play in all major aspects of the Church's life and ministry, whether internal to the Church or in outreach and service. We are a lay-centered Church whose membership is over 98 percent lay with less than 2 percent priests and religious. Collaboration in the mission of the Church is an essential responsibility of baptism. Many laity ignore this obligation, but a large number do not—a number that is well in excess of all priests and religious combined. While collaboration is often seen as priests and religious sharing their responsibility with laity, the opposite is more correct, for collaboration is rooted in baptism.

Increasing numbers of laity sacrifice themselves in Church-related jobs. They finance their own training, receive low pay and poor benefits, and have little or no opportunity for advancement. Some live collaboratively with no expectation of collaborative response from Church management. The Church of the next decade, while working to change these unacceptable circumstances, will need to capitalize on this generous ministry of laity.

The present situation of positive dedication of laity is the result of the ministry of priests and religious as well as laity. In the past, priests and religious trained, formed, educated, and delegated responsibility to laity. Now training, formation, education, and responsibility are the result of mutual interaction and are mutually beneficial—laity learning from other laity and priests and religious, while priests and religious learn from each other and from laity. The knowledgeable and gifted in Church life and ministry no longer correspond to a restricted vocational group. After all, laity have as much to contribute, but their contribution is different. They may not have studied theology, but they are in touch with valid theology at its roots.

The emergence of laity in the Church is not merely a Church phenomenon, but a reflection of the general evolution of society. It means the emergence of a new type of Church in which leadership and ministry are experienced and developed in new ways. Laity are discovering that being authoritative people of stature is more important than having authority. In fact, people who need to claim positions of authority generally do not carry authority among their followers.

Living in a lay-centered Church will require new styles of expressing the self-sacrifice of religious and priests. They are called to acknowledge the charisms of laity, reevaluate their relationship with laity, and develop a comprehensive plan for future collaboration with laity. They will also need to renounce certain types of delegation that give impressions of patronization or clericalism, as can happen when a pastor shares with laity only those ministries that he himself really does not want. We must all learn how to collaborate without monopolizing the tasks, the initiatives, or the policy making. Collaboration gives us the chance to portray a new image of the Church in which we gladly work with others, stifle no one, mutually empower each other, and capitalize on the competence of everyone. This will imply risk, some loss of control, and transitional conflict.

Although numbers of priestly and religious vocations are smaller, the number of men and women who dedicate themselves to ministry is increasing. Imagine what the Church could be like if this dedication is utilized, and imagine what it will be like if it is not. Those priests and religious who can channel the willing collaboration of laity will build up the Church, help the vocational fulfillment of laity, and also be faithful to their own call to serve the Church.

In some sections of the Church, collaboration will develop very slowly because distinctions between clergy and laity are still firmly drawn, structures are dominantly hierarchical, and there is fear of eroding the status associated with vocation. Moreover, many laity remain passive, like it that way, and will continue that way. Difficulties on all sides will remind us that nothing significant will be attained without a conversion through a paschal living of the cross of our Lord.

Spiritual Value of Collaboration

Neither personal fulfillment nor Christian ministry grow in isolation. Christian growth and ministry are always communal experiences. We realize our potential in communion with others. Thus, collaboration is a formative power that can generate individual spiritual growth and ecclesial vision. In fact, collaboration is a sign authenticating the theological life of faith, hope, and charity: faith because we believe God has gifted each one so much that we must capitalize on the gifts of all; hope because collaboration anticipates the growth we attain through interaction; charity because collaboration is only possible through the group's love for each other. Unfortunately, there is sometimes too little faith for the existence of a collaborative approach to ministry.

Christian collaboration is a form of ongoing discernment and is always carried out "in the Lord." It requires openness and detachment as one searches with others for the direction of the Lord; an attitude of constant attention and listening; and prayer that permeates the interactions of collaboration.

As Christians we do not collaborate merely as a way of being more efficient but rather as a way of living our faith. Thus, we prepare for collaboration as if approaching something sacred. We approach it with reflection and benevolence toward others; with social and political awareness that we can together achieve the common goals of our ministry; with spiritual readiness borne of a humble awareness that God alone gives growth and fulfillment. Collaboration needs patience as we struggle to share vision and work together for common goals. It needs prudence since not all are capable of discerning the truth the Lord brings to us through collaborative sharing. Collaborating with others requires courage—Christian fortitude—to challenge each other with frankness and honesty or to let go with genuine detachment.

Modern Christians can attain a more thoroughly developed spiritual life through the interdependence and coresponsibility experienced in collaboration. This working together, motivated by faith, prolongs Christian ministry, portrays an appealing image of the Church, and leads to spiritual maturity. Collaboration brings to the fore new leaders and critics with bright ideas—both of the utmost importance for the future vitality of any group.

Facilitating Collaboration

Collaboration takes place on different levels—intellectual, organizational, and personal. Depending on the team, one or another may need to be facilitated. Eventually all three levels must be integrated. This demands reasonable maturity from the members; a commitment to each other and to the common mission of the team; trust; and an appreciation of how each member contributes to the common goals of the team. Innovative companies are introducing collaborative administration, and ministers can do no less. Indeed, collaboration must be a goal of the team and a realistic expectation of each member.

Baptismal equality, like that manifested in collaboration, does not exclude the presence or need of exceptional leaders. However, those leaders could be priests, religious, or lay. Moreover, leadership is not equated with authority. Some people hold positions of authority, but actually carry no leadership among their peers or dependents. In the past leaders emerged and were given authority, now individuals are appointed to positions of authority and presumed to be leaders. Nowadays, exercising leadership as an authority figure requires different skills than formerly, since the tasks are more difficult and facilitating a communal response to mission is also more difficult.

Spiritual leadership includes many skills, one of which is to create a climate conducive to collaboration—a climate that will stimulate people to constantly pursue this goal of collaborative ministry. In our generation many church managers do not have these skills and although they remain in positions of authority their leadership is never authenticated by their people. For a spiritual leader, collaboration is the incarnation of faith, whereas authoritarianism, based as it is on self-sufficiency and rejection of the gifts of others, is the incarnation of doubt.

The role of leaders in collaborative ministry is also to acknowledge that the person in authority may not be the leader. This is especially the case with larger groups where individuals appointed to authority have struggled unsuccessfully to acquire leadership. Some organizations, such as universities, like parishes are notorious for their inability to adapt structures and are among the most autocratically governed organizations in any society. Their resistance to change makes the work of facilitating collaboration very difficult.

Besides acknowledging the differences between authority and leadership and the reluctance of autocratically governed institutions to change, leaders are conscious that people do not dedicate themselves to the work of a group that does not invite and welcome the contributions of all members. There is no commitment without participation. Moreover, followers quickly size up a new authority figure and rapidly decide whether he or she has collaborative leadership skills and, if not, they withdraw their support. When an authority figure generates collaboration in planning, implementation, evaluation, and change, that person's leadership is acknowledged and support assured.

One of the key components of a leadership that results from faith is the awareness that creative insights and concrete directives for the organization's future ministry do not filter down to the members, but percolate upward to authority figures. Leaders will facilitate this process without feeling any threat to their daily administration of the organization. A leader who is welcomed because of his or her collaborative vision and skills also feels quite at home and unthreatened in the fulfillment of the daily tasks of management. A commitment to collaboration is not a burden; in fact, it influences less than twenty percent of any manager's responsibilities. Those participating in a collaborative ministry are quite happy to leave each other alone in their daily work. Collaboration refers more to the discerning of areas of mission, role clarification, planning, major decision making, and evaluation.

A good leader collaborates with all members of an organization, but a great leader is one who knows how every member fits into the work of the organization. The great leader has a vision of community and collaborative ministry. Collaboration not only portrays a contemporary image of Church but also is a sign of exceptional leadership.

Treating Others as Partners

When leaders put themselves forward as officials in authority, they generally lose both their leadership and authority. In the best Christian communities, major decisions are arrived at by collaboration just as major areas of ministry are carried out collaboratively.

Recent studies have shown that today's best-run organizations are those where all participants are treated as adults, shown respect, and given the conviction that their role and views count. The ongoing sharing between leaders and followers guarantees the emergence of new leaders as needed. Some religious groups, having worked with laity for many years, are unconvinced that laity have the vision and knowledge to take over and continue their mission. Where this is so, it is due to very poor leadership in the religious group since one of the most basic qualities in leadership is the ability to clarify values, share a vision, and facilitate their integration by others.

Facilitating a dedication to collaboration in ministry, especially in cases where laity were previously excluded, is itself a spiritual journey for the leader. This is certainly what Jesus did with the Twelve, the Seventy-Two, and many individual disciples. Moreover, Jesus had no need of collaborative help since his ministry was small scale and restricted to a small region. Jesus' collaborative approach to ministry is imitated by the early Church in Acts.

Present problems in the Church, and perennial values of faith, demand that we develop a strong commitment to collaboration. This has its source in personal commitment rather than as the result of drifting toward change. It means learning to trust others deeply enough that we can communicate freely, work together pleasantly and caringly, serve each other, be demanding on each other, tap each other's talents, and pray with each other. It demands a capacity for authentic interpersonal relationships and an awareness of being a vital, active, and efficient member of the team.

Our creative fidelity to baptismal coresponsibility calls for a conversion to collaborative forms of administration and ministry. We cannot continue what went before but must grasp the opportunity that collaboration offers on the level of ecclesial and individual growth.

Initiating Collaboration

Initiating collaboration in any organization begins in one of two ways, both of which apply to the Church. The increase in collaborative ministry in the years ahead will require new skills in both the clerical leaders who remain and in the new lay leaders who emerge. This will imply a necessary refocusing of seminary education to include these new skills or new curricula in ministry programs for laity. One of these two ways is through the selection of leaders who have the vision and skills of collaboration. Such leaders act like talent scouts seeking the gifts of people and together with them create a new and compelling vision, develop commitment to the vision, and eventually institutionalize the vision. Each religious organization needs one or two pilot projects where gifted leaders can breathe life into a new vision of administration and ministry. These leaders will share their own distinctive charisms without threatening others, and they will receive the charisms of others and integrate them into a common vision without being threatened by them. These leaders will be courageous, knowing that too much caution is frequently indicative of a commitment to the status quo. Through initiating a collaborative vision they can resolve present needs in the Church, open to future developments, and prove the ongoing value and vitality of each one's insight and charism.

The second way for an organization to initiate collaboration is to be sensitive to the values and vision that percolate upward from the grass roots of any ecclesial group in which followers are dedicated and strive to be faithful to a shared vision. Such followers develop a feeling for the organization's charism without having formally expressed it or been trained in it. They develop a consensus for what is important and a corporate dedication to the organization's goals. In many religious groups, laity, without the encumbrances of major administrative responsibilities, are at the cutting edge of daily life where the spirit of the group is made relevant, passed on, and faithfully incarnated.

Some members of an organization have the leadership skills to initiate collaboration; others have the skills to listen, identify, and receive the dedication of collaborators. If collaboration in administration and ministry is seen as a dimension of Christian prophetical witness and is facilitated as a genuine discernment, then neither clergy, religious, nor laity need feel oppressed by the decisions made, since all are called to be docile to the Spirit in others.

Whether the approach be skilled leadership or response to followership, collaboration is first seen in commitment to common values. Without this we are working in a vacuum. A planning process is a good way to begin, provided it clearly affirms the contributions of everyone, confronts the contributions with the common charism of Christianity (and if necessary, the distinctive charisms of specific religious groups), and integrates the accepted ideas into a common vision that everyone can see they contributed to.

The common vision can then be condensed in goals attainable over a limited time. The organization, identifying the gifts of each member, assigns goals to individuals or subgroups so that everyone feels they are contributing and have a part to play in both the life of the group and its mission. This will include attention to the corporate character of the Church, the development of appropriate collaborative structures and skills, and a willingness to realize the vision at every level of Church life.

An essential component of collaboration is evaluation. This focuses on both the success of the mission and whether the ministry was not only carried out, but also carried out with the spirit of both the common Christian charism and the specific charism of individual religious groups. When priests, religious, and laity work together in common ministry, their baptismal dignity is equal, their ministry radically the same, and their accountability is mutual. Each vocation can learn from the others and challenge the others to greater fidelity in commitment.

Critical Issues in Collaboration

Forming Collaborative Groups

Spiritual life, when genuinely Christian, naturally leads to an enriching involvement with others. It is not necessary to plan one's involvement because, if our commitment to spiritual growth is deep enough, it will have an internal dynamic of its own that will lead us to others. However, it is useful to understand the psychological development of group life so that when involved with others in ministry we are aware of growth phases and problem phases in group life.

A group refers to any number of people from a minimum of about eight to a maximum of about thirty. In this chapter the concept of group includes both the small groups that develop within parishes for prayer or ministry purposes as well as the parish leadership teams, whether they include a priest or not. Moreover, these stages of psychological development can be verified in spontaneous groups of laity that organize themselves for ministry purposes. Christian development is essentially dependent on spiritual enrichment within such groups. In fact, originally Christianity was lived within small groups. Gathered around a local bishop, the community was a group that was small enough to allow a sharing of life and faith. As the bishop's community became larger, the Church soon appreciated its need to divide into smaller groups, and the priests were then authorized to celebrate the Eucharist for such groups. Now the parish group is in the same situation in which the bishop's community previously found itself. The strength of any large group or community is dependent on the strength of the smaller groups within it. Thus, a local parish draws its strength from the life of the small spiritual and apostolic groups that it fosters, and where these are lacking, weakness is clearly seen in parish life.

There are three essential elements for the life of a group: interpersonal relationships, common objective, and the interaction between these two. When these three are present, we move from occasional get-togethers of several people to a solid organized group. Moreover, when these elements are present, we have more than a simple socializing or a physical togetherness; instead we have a definite union of persons at depth.

The interpersonal relationships, at first superficial, gradually become personal and personalizing and aid each of the members in liberating themselves from defense mechanisms which block interpersonal growth. The common objective is some definite work of the group. Gradually the members become aware of their common aim and their own role in the task for the common good. In the life of the group there are dual emphases: the personal relationships and the common objective—a simultaneous growth of friendship and efficacy of work. These remove the concrete dangers of merely socializing on the one hand, or simply forming a work group on the other. When group members experience interaction between the deepening of interpersonal relationships and the strengthening of a common objective, then each one appreciates that he or she has something to give and to receive both on the level of action and on the level of life.

Why does a person join a group? First, each individual person will only come to a desire to develop group life if the group is seen as a benefit. This is not just selfishness but the psychological reason for the formation of a group. Group life is seen as a reality that can satisfy personal needs. If it is not seen in this way, then a group will never form. Many people do not involve themselves in parish life because the parish is not seen as satisfying their needs. Some live in religious communities, but they do not see the community as satisfying basic psychological needs, and so they never really belong to it even though they live in it. Second, people enter group life because they see it satisfies a personal need for liberation (in a religious sense, redemption). One of the great threats that everyone faces is isolation, but the group offers to liberate us from this and to fulfill our personal aspirations. This basic need is a force that draws and integrates members of a group. In addition, everyone faces certain social frustrations and the group is seen as offering the possibility of overcoming these, or at least of reducing them to a minimum by offering a new synthesis that leads to the social adaptation we need. Third, The group must be known to be a group that will respect individuality and allow each member to develop it. Members need to be assured that they will not simply be absorbed. No one is drawn to a group unless it is seen as letting each person express his or her own originality. Fourth, there must be a proportion between the efforts needed in group life and the probability of attaining results expected from the group's development. No one will pay more than the goods are worth! This does not mean a decrease in generosity. Psychologically a person must see the possibility that these basic needs will be satisfied before he or she can be involved.

Phases of Group Growth

What is said here is true of any group, but our concern is with a group whose members are committed to each other in order to develop Christian life. To unite people in groups, one cannot start out from prefabricated schemes but from concrete existential situations. Each individual has his or her own list of values, experiences, and motivations. However, there are several underlying aspirations in all of us, and where these are satisfied, a group will be born. Once the group is together, the common internal forces at play offer certain patterns in development. The phases of growth in any group can be considered as the following: (1) the moment of coming together, (2) the phase of human relationships, (3) a period of maturing of the ideal of the group, (4) a period of consolidation in the maturity of the group, and (5) the permanence or division of the group.

For Christians it is enlightening to note that these various stages are similar to those used in Christian initiation by the early Church: (1) moment of proclamation—the *kerygma*, (2) period of evangelization, (3) the catechumenate leading to baptism, (4) period of post-baptismal formation—the *mystogogia*, and (5) moment of union in the Eucharist. Let us now consider each of these stages in the dynamic growth of a group.

1. *The group is born.* What brings together people with common aspirations? We must start with concrete situations, for that which brings people together will be a fact that arises from normal daily living. However, it is not just a simple fact, but rather a special event that in its own way constitutes a profoundly human and religious experience. It will be a clearly defined goal of real value to all the members, an intuition that several share. They then realize that this intuitive vision can be attained and made real precisely by the permanence of these same "visionaries" in a stable group. In a broad sense, this moment of insight can be appreciated as a liberating, redemptive, and salvific event. For those who reflect on it, this special group appreciation or group intuition is a first discovery of the basic Christian truth that salvation is experienced in community.

The first stage in group development, the convocation, can come about simply by chance, or it can be provoked. It could be an appeal for specific help or the launching of a definite service for the benefit of people in a given area. On the other hand, it could be the result of a mission in the parish or a renewal course. Out of the congregation, a small number decide to live more intensely what has been proclaimed to them. They see they are not alone, appreciate the common vision, feel a sense of solidarity, and know the aim is to be achieved by these few staying together. On reflection, this coming together for life and common work is seen as the result of an acceptance of an aspect of Christian proclamation. The awareness of the need to be and to grow together is one of the demands of the Christian faith, and the promotion of this awareness is one of the functions given to apostolic groups by the Second Vatican Council.

2. *The phase of human relationships.* After the initial event, there follows some kind of life together through meetings and the like. There follows, too, the need to be together to clarify the first understanding of the group's aim. This social interaction fosters a sense of solidarity. At first some local need may be the expressed reason for being together, but gradually trust and friendship grow, and the members feel more and more drawn to share their own personal problems in the hope that the group can help in their solution. This is a period when one hopes to receive from the group. However, individuals already appreciate some of the demands of group life, such as respect for other people, lived equality, the principle of subsidiarity, which urges delegation to the

lowest levels of a group, and a sense of coresponsibility in the pursuit of the common good.

As sharing increases through the promotion of Christian friendship, truly human values, discussion and dialogue, the members become more sensitive to the needs of the group and become aware of the balance that can exist between real belonging or identification and a genuine sense of self-direction, between an ability to collaborate and an ability to live out one's own role. Then, too, they appreciate and experience that group growth does not mean conformism or absorption. At this period, life values become more significant than individualistic needs, and so it is important for the group to discover Christ and the values he gives to life. This is the moment of evangelization and of confrontation of life with the gospel.

This phase lasts a certain time, shorter or longer depending on the maturity of the members and the intensity of the community side of life. If the group only meets infrequently, the stage will develop slowly. If the meetings or get-togethers are frequent and the sharing deep, then the stage will be short.

However, once the early stages have passed, the group enters into a phase of crisis in their human relationships, generally based on the fact that some feel that the whole focus of the group's life is too demanding for them. Differences are more evident between members, and some feel the weight of demands that life with others makes on them. For this type of life, a person needs self-perception and self-acceptance; a capacity for authentic interpersonal relationships; the will to live in the love of Christ; and an attitude of living as a part, as one who can be an integrated, active, and efficient member of the group. Some cannot manage all this, and they see that they must change. Many begin to ask what really brought them together, and the succeeding discussion of more important life problems shows up the weakness of those who are just there for the socializing.

Those who simply want to remain on the socializing level generally withdraw from the group at this time. This is a painful period filled with the tension between the will to continue in the group and the defense of one's own way of life. The tension can last for months. However, the crisis can be overcome as each one begins to search with the others for the true direction of his or her personal life and for the direction of the life of the group.

3. *A period of maturing of the ideal of the group.* The common search for direction in life opens a phase of systematic reflection. The group organizes more meetings on the Christian mystery, confronts members' own experiences with the ideal of Christian life, and commits itself more and more to attain this ideal. This phase is like the catechumenate of the early Church with all its tests and discussions, culminating in an awareness and living of the baptismal commitment. It is a period of great Christian challenge when the members can develop from babes to spiritual adults (cf. 1 Cor. 3:1–4).

During this period the group will still have a definite leader, and his or her job is to lead the group to the discovery of the ideal before it, without having all the answers. The leader needs to animate and coordinate, to establish deep relationships with each person and, where necessary, recall the group to its ideal, especially through personal example.

Right from the early period of being together the group has had a common aim. However, as yet there has been no common way of achieving it, and, as the members work together, they come up against differences in each member's way of doing things. This is a period of second crisis that challenges the groups' commitment to each other.

Other leaders now arise to get the work done, but then it is not the work of the group. The members now appreciate the need for all to have an active share in the work, life, and direction of the group. However, it is a period of strain and can be more painful than the first crisis period because the ties between the members are now stronger. The pain experienced at this time can lead to growth, or it can also be a time of division within the group because the rhythms of maturing are different. Charity may necessitate setting up two groups or structures for varied rhythms of growth within the group.

4. *A period of consolidation.* The second crisis is overcome with the discovery of the profound power of dialogue and of an understanding that group growth is achieved through the death of the parts. This is a period of group growth and maturity through a deepened awareness of the contributions of all in the group, whether inspirers, visionaries, organizers, doers, planners, or evaluators; through the consolidation of simple structures to guarantee a deeper sharing (shared prayer, communication of life, revision of life, group discernment, group planning); through a development of the social-

izing dimensions as a way of renewing and sustaining the group. It is a period where union grows, not through excluding those who disagree, but rather through openness to the prophetic challenge that can frequently come from the nonconformists of the group.

This period of action within the group to give it more life is complemented with action outside the group. Although an apostolic or common work dimension has been present to the group since its formation, the point of focus now is that group growth leads to an understanding that the group's work or mission is no longer to do several things, but rather to achieve one thing, namely witness through the quality of the group's Christian life.

To help the group attain its mission of witnessing to a genuine Christian life, the group needs continually to renew itself and to form itself, and particularly new members, for ministry. To avoid becoming insular or ghettoized, it needs to be continually open to the efforts of other groups and to cooperate with them. To be sacrament of the world and offer Christian relevancy to people, the group will frequently have to revise its life together in confrontation with the gospel. Finally, to be prophetic, the group will have to be open to adaptation and ever new forms of living out the gospel message.

5. *The permanence or division of the group.* With the passing of time, new areas of action arise and, urged on by the love of Christ, the group wishes to respond to the needs it finds. Moreover if the group is a genuine sign and witness to others, it will have attracted others into its ranks, and new leaders will also have arisen. There follows a further crisis with the possible need to divide or establish subgroups. This crisis is the result of fullness, and any resulting division is not painful, but leads to a form of communion and a gift of life for others—Eucharist.

The author of the Letter to the Hebrews, speaking of group life and group asceticism, says: "Let us be concerned for each other, to stir a response in love and good works. Do not stay away from the meetings of the community, as some do, but encourage each other to go" (Heb. 10:24–25). Genuine Christian living essentially includes the development of life and of apostolic involvement within the group. To achieve this, members need to accept the daily grind of meetings and group practices. An initial common desire will bring the group together, but then the interplay of human forces gives rise to growth patterns we need to know, understand, and work through. It is to help us in this work of building that we have considered the phases of group growth.

Do you belong to a Christian group? What makes it Christian? What is the difference between its life now and a year ago? Which phase of group growth do you think your group is in? Could it be guided to a deeper stage of relationship? How long have you belonged to a prayer group? Is it exclusively a prayer group? Why? Does the group ever revise its own life together? Do you not think the group would benefit by developing other manifestations of Christian group life, even by healthy socializing? If it is large, as many prayer groups are, would it not achieve renewed youth and vigor if it divided?

Who are the people who are really important to you now? If none of them belongs to the basic group you live in, then maybe something is wrong. The asceticism of today is group asceticism in which individuals find the greatest possible enrichment in Christ. This group growth, like individual personal growth, has definite identifiable phases of development. Knowing where we are helps us to understand and guide our group growth.

Models of Collaboration

The Church's dedication to collaboration is not seen in teachings, but in the actions of ministers and Church officials who make sure that collaborative structures and policies are in place in the areas of their responsibility. Collaboration requires an asceticism, a willingness to risk and compromise, and a deep friendship based on faith. It is a contemporary witness to the deep union, *koinonia,* spoken of in the Acts of Apostles as the life that results from a faithful acceptance of the Holy Spirit. There are several models of collaboration in use, among them the following. I have used some simple diagrams to represent the varied forms of collaboration. The circle symbolizes collaborative sharing, the triangle symbolizes autocratic government. Thus, a circle within a triangle symbolizes a local collaborative structure within a larger autocratically governed one. The very small circles indicate members of the groups, presumed to be lay, while the shaded small circles indicate a member representative of the hierarchy.

Collaborative Team

- All members, whether lay, religious, or clergy, share in vision, administration, and faith.
- Although having individual responsibilities, the ministry of each is part of the corporate ministry of the team.
- Each member is responsible for, involved in, or informed about all projects.
- Responsibility and accountability are mutual.
- Meetings are time-consuming, and conflict is handled creatively.
- Each member has support systems outside the team to complement the support received from the team.

Collaboration with a Pastoral Leader

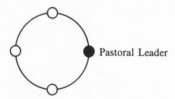

Pastoral Leader

- One member retains and exercises authority received from position.
- This form of collaboration is collegial since the group finds its realization and purpose in the one key figure.
- The pastoral leader is delegated by the bishop and responsible to the bishop for the ministry of the team.
- The pastoral leader is frequently a cleric who is dedicated to collaboration with parish team and parishoners.
- This demands a serious spiritual commitment by the one in charge. Collegiality is essentially a spirituality by which the one in charge finds his or her greater self in the discerned opinions of the team.
- This faith-filled collaborative approach is a specifically Christian form of structure and administration.
- This is maintained by fostering a collegial spirit in all the members

Corporate Ministry

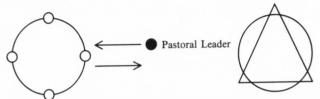

Pastoral Leader

- The Code of Canon Law allows for a corporate pastorate of laity with a priest supervisor.
- The pastor supervises the corporate pastorate on behalf of the bishop. It is not stated that the priest is actually part of the team, but he could be.
- The Code envisions the pastoral leader as a priest endowed with the powers and faculties of a pastor to supervise the pastoral care of the parish (see Canon 517, 2).
- The priest-supervisor sees to it that tasks are done, but the code gives no suggestions as to how he does this.
- The key issue is how this new form of pastorate is interpreted.
- One pastor says, "we empower each other to exercise our gifts, and follow each other as each one leads in his or her area of giftedness."

Interparochial or Interdiocesan Collaboration of Peers

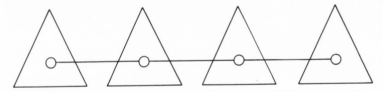

- When there is no local team, individuals should still provide a collaborative structure through peers in other parishes or dioceses.
- This can take place when individuals work on their own but capitalize on the support, challenge, experience, and vision of other ministers.
- This can be especially important when each individual works within a local church that is dominantly hierarchical, possibly overmanaged, and underled.
- This mutual support may be necessary when an authority figure has all the post–Vatican II vocabulary while still manifesting the attitudes and convictions of the fifties.

Collaborative Ministry within Autocratic Structures

- A team can live collaboratively even though it is within a rigidly hierarchical structure that may live autocratically.
- The team gains ministerial support to endure life and possibly oppression from the larger structure.
- The team can relate pleasantly and politely to the larger structure while never affirming its autocratic style.

Collaborative Ministry within a Presumed Collaborative Structure That is Known to be Autocratic

- This can be interesting, at times amusing, and also educationally significant.
- The collaborative team lives within an autocratic structure but acts as if the authority figures in the structure are collaborative.
- Thus they act collaboratively towards the authorities without expecting collaborative style in return.
- This simple form of behavior modification acts on the presumption that collaboration will be shown.

Collaborative Couple

- Although included in one or other of the above models, the collaborative ministry of married couples is a significant form of ministry today.

- This collaboration requires similar qualities to those already mentioned but must also be assured of a healthy sexual life for the spouses without which the effectiveness of the ministry will end.

Collaborative Team within a Collaborative Structure

- This can be particularly challenging since it is sometimes easier to mold a collaborative approach when threatened from outside by autocratic oppression.
- As the team treats each other so will the members of the larger group treat each other.

Collaboration and False Opposition

- Sometimes a team that works collaboratively thinks of and treats the surrounding structure as autocratic even if it is not.
- This negative formational influence is unhealthy for the team.
- When possible, the team should respond positively to the surrounding structure by reinforcing collaborative gestures whenever they appear.

Partial Collaboration

- The vision of collaboration may be accepted but the sharing is incomplete and inadequate.
- This sometimes indicates a team that had the vision of collaboration but not the appropriate skills.

Working in a Noncollaborative Structure

One author who referred to collaboration as the "queen of Vatican II's achievements" concluded that it is "now a sleeping princess." Expressing the hope that "some day her prince will come" needs to be tempered with the awareness that there is a tendency to let collaboration gather dust, a tendency that seems to receive official international support. There are available escape routes used by those who wish to avoid accepting a collaborative approach to government and ministry. It is easy to give intellectual assent to the call to collaboration, but we still resist when it means changing our lives.

Collaboration is an attitude of mind and heart, a true conversion to a major aspect of Christianity's vision. It is a pilgrimage in faith, hope, and love, but, like all journeys, it starts very simply and needs time to reach its goal. We need patience but a sense of urgency too.

Signs of Noncollaboration

- Although laity share in the mission of the Church, they rarely participate in decision making.
- Asked to serve on parish and diocesan councils, the contribution is merely consultative.
- The input of lay ministers has not been adequately sought for the Synods on Family and Laity.
- Many lay ministers isolate themselves from their own colleagues and peers.
- The lay version of clericalism, namely staffism, is frequently experienced.
- Some parishioners have expressed concern about oligarchies of angry laity in their parishes.
- Openness to outside communities in ecumenical matters is sometimes greater than communion within the Church.

Please add signs from your own experience.

Responses to Noncollaboration

- Realize we are in paradigmatic change with all the anxieties such a shift brings.
- Accept some painful experiences that are transitional correctives.
- Remember single-minded dedication easily becomes stubbornness.
- Be aware that compromise rarely renews.
- Cultivate a creative tolerance towards those who cannot adapt to collaboration.
- Do not participate in autocratic structures; participation will encourage and confirm inadequate exercises of authority.
- Avoid all forms of violence to others in word, criticism, and reputation.
- If differences in the team are extreme, it is advisable to leave where possible.

Please add other responses to noncollaboration that you have found helpful.

Topics for Reflection and Discussion

Personal Questions on Collaboration

1. Are you a dialogic person?
2. If you are experiencing noncollaborative responses, are they results of personality clashes or do they have a structural character?

3. Are you hopeful of solution through struggle?
4. Can you appreciate other member's models of ministry and government?
5. Are you collaborative with volunteers who work with you?
6. Do you delegate whenever possible?
7. Is this struggle an integral part of your spiritual life?

Please add other significant questions and issues concerning collaboration that you wish to reflect on.

Questions for Group Sharing

1. Most groups react and change under pressure. To what extent do your groups anticipate changes and plan for collaborative responses?
2. If collaboration is a part of an authentic Christian vision, it should be confirmed by experience. How does your experience support the values of collaboration?
3. What is the relationship between growth in faith and growth in collaboration? How do you experience this?
4. Which Church-related structures are the most difficult to change? Why do you think they are?
5. Since many Church-related organizations are run by religious orders, what is the relationship between religious obedience and collaboration?
6. What is the role of authority in a collaborative vision?
7. Who were the most dedicated people you knew when you last worked in a Church-related institution? Are they still there? Are they in leadership positions? Have they left? If so, for what reason?
8. How do you see the Church in ten years time? As centralized as now or decentralized?
9. Do you think the future Church will be authoritarian or collaborative in administration? Would such a shift be approved by Vatican administrators? If so, why? If not, why not?

10. Christianity, like other religions, is based on revealed Scriptures authoritatively interpreted by hierarchical agencies. It claims revelation, inspiration, and canonicity for its books. Can an organization with such a history of centralized authority accept collaboration?

Some Concerns about Collaboration Expressed by Lay Ministers

As a married woman in the parish eighteen years, I served on the staff two years with three priests, and only one ever really respected my input.

•

Sometimes too many cooks in the soup, more people make logistics difficult, actions are slower to evolve.

•

The training itself needs to be collaborative. One must have an internship with priests who want to work with laity.

•

The team model is written about and talked about, but I wonder how successful it really is. Our parish is trying the collaborative model, and we have a long way to go to reach real collaboration.

•

It is hard to find a whole team whose ecclesiologies, priorities, and vision are all similar, whose methods and styles are compatible, and who like each other! Another obstacle is people who say they use the team approach but actually do not.

•

True collaboration is so foreign to most people's experience that there is need to begin defining collaboration and explaining how to collaborate. Then it is a matter of learning by example.

Selected Reading

Boff, Leonardo. *Church: Charism and Power.* New York: Crossroad, 1985.
Doohan, Leonard. *Laity's Mission in the Local Church: Setting a New Direction.* San Francisco: Harper & Row, 1986.

McKenzie, L. *Decision Making in Your Parish: Effective Ways to Consult the Local Church.* West Mystic, CT: Twenty-Third Publications, 1980.

Power, David N. *Gifts that Differ: Lay Ministries Established and Unestablished.* New York: Pueblo, 1980.

Whitehead, Evelyn Eaton, and James D. Whitehead. *The Emerging Laity.* New York: Doubleday & Co., Inc., 1986.

Additional Reading

Doohan, Leonard. *The Laity: A Bibliography.* Wilmington, DE: Michael Glazier, Inc., 1987. See sections 15, 16, 26, 28, 29, 39.

Chapter 3

WORKING TOGETHER: IMPLICATIONS OF A COLLABORATIVE MINISTRY

L̲ay Ministers Speak on Working Together

Reflections

Introduction
New Models of Ministry
Training for Working Together
A Climate That Fosters Working Together
Forces Against Working Together in Ministry
Support Systems for Those Who Work Together
Institutionalizing the Vision

Critical Issues in Working Together

Sharing Life
Planning for Common Work
Evaluations

Topics for Reflection and Discussion

Is Your Team a Caring Group?
Questions for Group Sharing

Some Concerns about Working Together Expressed by Lay
Ministers

Selected Reading

Lay Ministers Speak on Working Together

I was prepared for working together in ministry by growing up in a family where decisions were made together, and our ideas were accepted as valid by our parents, and by working in a university in laboratory research where you must work together if experiments are to be successful.

•

I think all ministries are complementary. Some people are good with children, some with teens, some with adults, some with the troubled, some with the liturgy—together we minister to whole lives.

•

Seeing the faith of others, learning what it means to be accepting of others and where they are at, witnessing how God works in our brokenness, in our weakness, and often in spite of us, enhances our appreciation of the opportunity to work together. The challenge to face the truths within oneself, to face one's own poverty is invaluable to growth and authentic love and compassion.

•

Working together we need a desire to grow spiritually, an understanding and compassion for others, an ability to forgive and reconcile, patience and gentleness, a willingness to listen, and an ability to share one's own story and to listen to others' stories.

•

I see my ministry as twofold: being a source of information, encouragement, and leadership, and also as a role model for other lay people, especially women.

Reflections

Introduction

We have seen the history of ministry and current emphasis on a vision of the Church that implies collaboration in knowledge, ministry, and sharing. Recent history has led to this changed focus, and the Church seeks to respond anew as it did in the past. The vision of a collaborative Church leads to many practical implications in the way we work with each other in a day-to-day shared ministry. This vision came with the Second Vatican Council, and this chapter focuses on the practical results of this vision.

The Second Vatican Council in its document on laity insisted that the Christian vocation is essentially a vocation to ministry (Laity 2:1). It affirmed that laity are sharers in the priestly, prophetic, and royal office of Christ (Laity 2:2; 10:1) and derive the right to minister directly from Christ himself (Laity 3:1; 4:1) who personally assigns them to minister and supports them through the sacraments (Laity 3:1). Laity exercise their apostolate both in the Church and in the world (Laity 5:1; 9:1). The success of their work depends upon their union with Christ (Laity 4:1), with each other, and especially with their pastors (Laity 3:3). In fact, they should exercise their ministry by way of a united effort (Laity 18:2).

Although the laity's ministry is considered indispensable (Laity 10:1), and they are referred to as "fellow-workers for the truth" (3 John 8), there remains in conciliar teachings an important distinction between the apostolate of the laity and pastoral ministry (Laity 6:1). Conciliar teachings on lay ministry are exceptionally positive, but there are two presuppositions retained throughout the documents. The first is that laity's principal sphere of ministry is carried out in secular circumstances. This alone is their exclusive domain. The second presupposition is that whenever laity minister in Church matters, for example, through liturgical participation, community building, parish, or diocesan ministries, they work under the authority of the clergy. In secular matters, they are on their own, a leavening presence to the world. In ecclesiastical matters, they are instrumental to the hierarchy's ministry. Delegated and authorized through an ecclesiastical mandate, they "are fully subject to higher ecclesiastical direction in the performance of such work" (Laity 24:3). Neither position suggests that clergy and laity work together in collaborative leadership.

The Vatican Council's major insights and teachings were ecclesiological not ministerial, sacramental, or moral. Its teachings on ministry lagged behind its ecclesiology, and in places the teachings on lay ministry seem little influenced by the vision of the Church as community. In post-Council years we have seen interaction between the various strands of conciliar teaching, and its insights on lay ministry have been deepened by confronting them with the Council's own ecclesiological vision. As a result, laity are now more aware of the implications of baptismal commitment; they see that being Church is the distinguishing characteristic of their lives; they sense responsibility for their local Church; they have a new relationship with their clergy; they see themselves as ministers rather than objects of ministry; they resonate with the Council's statement that laity are living instruments of the mission of the entire Church (Church 33:2). Therefore no minister should feel alone nor merely one in an aggregate, rather all are part of the communion of the Church. As the Council's ecclesiology progressively enriches its teachings on ministry, we move to new models of ministry, shape and mold our ministry in new ways, appreciate our growing interdependence, and find that working together in collaborative leadership is the way both to participate in and attain the vision of our Church as communion.

New Models of Ministry

Changes since the Council have provoked a series of crises in role clarification for priests, religious, and laity. In the use of vocabulary to describe the laity's work—is it charism, service, apostolate, or ministry?—and in the description given to the manager of the community—is he priest, minister, pastor, or leader? Although Jesus presented ministry as universal and ecclesial, its development was restricted and ecclesiastical. Although the faithful yearn for sacramental life, increasing numbers are deprived of the sacraments. Although the faithful are equal in baptism, the clergy are still seen as a privileged class. At a time when many laity are involved in Church services, and many clergy and religious are involved in social and political ventures, we hear reference to the clericalization of laity and the laicization of the clergy and religious.

The crises have become a concentrated challenge to Christians to participate in their Church in new ways, and a consensus is emerging that we need new models of ministry to creatively respond to the crises. Sadly we acknowledge that some of the hierarchy are not in the vanguard of this movement, and some clergy, religious, and laity portray an institutional fundamentalism, a philosophy of conformity to the status quo. For such fundamentalists, disagreement is always seen negatively. The result has been the development of parallel structures of ministry, or the development of collaborative structures alongside the hierarchically controlled forms. Thus we have teachers who leave parish schools and continue their ministry in nonecclesiastically controlled schools. We see priests incardinated in a diocese but freelancing in ministry outside the control of their own diocesan structures. We have grown accustomed to the spontaneous and creative ministries of religious who live on their own, carrying out a ministry they have personally developed outside of ecclesiastical controls.

It is especially in outreach service to the secular that we have seen the largest regrouping in ministry. Laity, many of whom were trained in ecclesiastically controlled spiritual movements, now spontaneously develop an explicit ministry dimension to their professions; doctors, teachers, business people, parents. While rejecting the designation of volunteers, others give a portion of their time to bring an explicitly Christian dimension to the work for peace, alleviation of hunger, cultural development, and justice. This dedicated service to human need is achieved by husband-wife teams, small spontaneous groups, mobile teams of ministers, groups in a religious community, and participants in spiritual movements. Primarily the ministry is team ministry and generally loosely structured.

Internal to parishes and dioceses we also find new forms of dedication to ministry. Several parishes use the parish council as an occasion to live collaborative ministry; other parishes have pastors who see themselves as inspirers and liturgical leaders to many apostolic groups within their community. Some dioceses have developed intervocational teams to minister to superparishes, clusters of parishes, or widespread rural areas. Priestless parishes have ministry teams made up of teachers, organizers, planners, and administrators. Some active parishes have developed a great variety of teams to deal with prayer, hospitality, charitable activities, right-to-life issues, sanctuary, fund raising, mourning of the community's dead, hunger, youth work, healing ministries, and family needs.

There are many laity who have no interest in ministry. There are many religious and priests whose ministry is cosmetic. Nevertheless, dedication to ministry is becoming a part of the lives of many Christians. The total picture of the Church's ministry is very different than it was before the Council. Now it is predominantly lay, organized in groups, directed to world needs, and at the cutting edge of issues judged significant by modern men and women.

New models of ministry can help us move to a new understanding of the Church. When we are all dedicated to a spirit of service, and when many give some or all of their time to a professional service of others, when we have ceased to view ourselves as volunteers, when we are mutually supportive of each other's ministry, when we share our ministry and bring others forward to new ministries, then we are shaping our Church in a new way. We have the task of challenging our Church to make its structures more collaborative, and ministers should ask themselves what cooperative ventures they have initiated for working together.

New models of ministry must also be prophetic in achieving the implications of an understanding of the Church as community by living out shared responsibility in areas of planning, decision making, and overall policy. We will need to be creative in finding alternatives to current impasses that result from Canon Law, historical and political developments, role confusion, and fear.

Training for Working Together

Training for ministry is shaped by ecclesiology. Although we have a new vision of Church, the training for ministry has lagged behind this vision. Large numbers of Church leaders have been trained, and still are trained, to work in a Church governed on a pyramid model in which the clerical manager is presumed to be the leader, even though leadership skills are rarely included in seminary training. Many clerics are natural leaders and have quickly adapted to collegial and collaborative styles of leadership. They have been able to achieve this even when their congregations have been reluctant to do so. Other pastors do not have collaborative skills, and either rely on the diplomatic skills learned in seminary or acquired from their peers. Some adopt a laissez-faire style which quickly degenerates into chaos, or in fear they retrogress to autocratic styles of government. Lack of collaborative skills in leadership is a problem faced not only by seminary students but by religious and laity too, many of whom are trained for ministry in traditional seminaries or seminary consortia.

Among the convictions that form part of every minister's vision is the awareness that there are no essential distinctions in Church members, all of whom entered the Church through the sacrament of freedom. All the baptized are both teachers and learners. All are called to embody a spirit of service, and many to ministries in the Church, as part of the servant Church. All are mutually accountable to each other in both the organization of their local Church and its outreach in ministry. Together they are the celebrants of liturgy and builders of community life.

Building one's vision of Church in a local community by working together with others requires specific attitudes and skills, some of which are spiritual qualities, others of which are practical aids to group development. Ministry is not the sharing of one's abundance but rather a problem-posing ministry that lets the group be creative, liberating, and mutually educative.

How do you get everyone involved and still get something done? Ministers must first commit themselves to communities in which there are no extremes of views between the pastoral team and the people, or among members of the pastoral team. Extreme differences lead only to frustration, and there is little hope of a successful outcome in a common vision.

Ministers' training needs to include listening skills: constant attention to others and to God's call in them, an active listening that responds to others' wishes, an art of listening that joyfully and confidently believes that God's presence and will are discerned in community dialogue. This active listening includes a willingness to surround oneself with people better qualified that oneself and not feel threatened by them but rejoice in the team's strength.

Listening not only builds the confidence of the community but leads to a sharing of responsibility. Working with others requires that tasks be accomplished at the lowest level of the community's structure. Leaders should not do what can be done by followers. In practice we do not need to know what the lowest level is; all we need to do is delegate to followers closest to us, and the rest will take care of itself. This leadership from behind allows other more gifted people to come forth. Moreover, the sharing of responsibility, which ideally includes decision making, planning, and evaluation, is best initiated by working together—by doing something together before making decisions together.

Working together in ministry inevitably includes conflicts, but ministry preparation needs to include training for nondominant responses—conflict resolution without claiming the authority of position. Ministry teams need to be able to speak honestly to each other, confront and challenge each other, dialogue, and correct each other when necessary. Growth in collaboration will not be possible if someone in the team cannot handle conflict maturely. Conflict well handled will be a source of creative growth in the team for the benefit of the community.

Ministers should not be aggressive toward team members but assertive as occasion requires. This prophetic witness will include a spirit of confidence and freedom to go public with one's ideas. The team allows the critical evaluation of personal and communal experience.

Ministers need singlemindedness in their search for authentic Church life. They must be ready for persecution, even from other Christians, and be men or women of compassion and peace. Since they do not bring a ready-made Church to their followers but try to discern and discover it in the people, they will need both simplicity and detachment. They must be people of hope, vigilance, and prayer.

Collaboration requires ability to share one's vision, hopes, dreams, and experiences. Teams that are comfortable in sharing their faith and feelings generate trust and freedom of spirit. All involved in collaboration require perseverance both to build up their team spirit and to implement the common vision.

A Climate That Fosters Working Together

Working together in a team is not merely a more efficient approach to ministry but a way of living as a small cell of Church life. It is supported by the daily gestures of sharing, caring, mutual commitment, and quality presence to each other. Human qualities of loyalty, sincerity, and truthfulness are a foundation that can be enriched by interpersonal skills. Personal and personalizing relationships make the team a pleasant place to live and work. This means staying together long enough to develop deep and lasting relationships and team unity. It requires patience from everyone, clarity regarding the specific roles of each one, and mutual interest in the contributions that each can make to the collaborative commitment.

Teams spend time in study together, participate in the same courses, and read similar books as aids to the development of a common vision. Learning is not only professionally necessary, but can fuel the life of the team. Moreover, the mutual experience of competence deepens confidence in each other. The team then shares a common background to discern God's presence and challenging grace.

Ministers should be challenging to each other, but magnanimous too. They should be willing to be flexible in order to avoid adversarial roles. In this context each one's freedom of conscience is respected, and love is maintained even when dissent is present in the team.

Those who collaborate in ministry can create an atmosphere of support by praying for each other's ministry, spending time together in retreat, and celebrating liturgy together.

A group's mutual love can be seen in not demanding more of some than of others, in being sensitive to feelings of insecurity and threat that some team members might face, in assuring team members of our quality presence to them, in joyfully welcoming individuals' new charisms, in helping each one evaluate their ministry, and in being part of the ongoing formation of each one. True love sometimes shows itself in opposition that helps keep others in touch with their essential mission by forcefully challenging them to reexamine their ministry.

Successful working together is fostered when ministers respect each other's dignity and respect each other's need for privacy, time alone, and leisure. Ministry is only a part of life, and one's colleagues must be assured of opportunities to develop friendships, family life, and social interests outside the ministry. Collaborative ventures that become all-absorbing and time-consuming can be valuable in the short run, but can lead to burnout and ineffectiveness in ministry in the long run.

Awareness that ministry is being done by many people, spontaneously or in organized groups, is a valuable contribution to a healthy climate for collaboration. Although the team may work full-time, many of the followers are no less professional in their work simply because they are part-time. Appreciation of others' gifts and dedication helps keep the team's own commitment in perspective and leads to a healthy and respectful approach to others.

Forces against Working Together in Ministry

People who live and work closely together are often poles apart. Collaborative ministry suffers from a series of tensions that frustrate the effectiveness of team ministry. About 59 percent of all those who work in ministry have no job description. This leads to the added difficulties of role clarification in teams. Particularly laity suffer from lack of placement opportunities and of financial support for ongoing training. If the cleric in the team wishes to use the current power of his position, then the team can effectively lack freedom of speech, have an artificial sharing of responsibility, and the nonclerics be seen as the extended arm of the hierarchy. These difficulties are intensified by the new code's insistence that nonclerical contributions be seen as merely consultative.

On a practical level, lay members of a team need further clarification of their role and call. Often the faithful do not know what to do with them and in some cases are slow to accept lay leadership. The security of the team is weakened by poor salaries and some of the less-than-desirable employment practices of the Church. Mutual trust is difficult in these cases, and working intervocationally becomes even more difficult when nonclerics see the Vatican seeking greater autocratic control, actively searching for a decrease in collaboration, and attempting to restore clerical dominance. At times we seem to have a double Church and parallel ministries—a situation that leads to particularly delicate problems when the noncleric is better qualified than the cleric. The latter can become threatened and return to autocratic and oppressive approaches that destroy all possibility of collaboration.

When members of a team have very different understandings of the Church, different psychological or sociological reactions to collaborators and followers, and different approaches to ecclesiastical structure, it is inadvisable to pursue cooperation in a ministry venture. Likewise if any team member is clearly pursuing careerism, or the establishment of a private kingdom, or is paternalistic or maternalistic to colleagues, it is better for the others to withdraw.

Cooperation is weakened when members become excessively discouraged by their inability to change structures, when they are reduced to being task or project directors, and become paralyzed by insurmountable obstacles. The team likewise suffers when members have no job description or multiple job descriptions, or when they accumulate roles or are assigned incompatible objectives.

The team's ability to work together will always be weak if it lacks knowledge of group development—their own team's or their followers; if they are unable to deal with tension, ambiguity, criticism, and negativity; if they cannot motivate others; or if they have narrow criteria for success.

Some of these problems can lead to situational depression and eventually to burnout, a problem that affects the best and ultimately drives them away from ministry.

Some problems met in working together are never handled. Some teams simply mutually tolerate each others views; the decision of one is accepted today because someone else's will be accepted tomorrow. Other groups dialogue endlessly and rarely get anything done. Where a pastor may withdraw to allow a team freedom, we sometimes find that a former clericalism is replaced by staffism, and the nonclerical members of a team seem to see themselves as the Church's new office bearers.

Teams sometimes yield to the temptation to reduce to the lowest common denominator. This is particularly true regarding study but also regarding personal prayer and negative attitudes to authority. Ministers should avoid predispositions to conflict that set up the constant desire to "win."

Team ministry is difficult given the historical accumulation of power by the hierarchy. Personnel who have exalted opinions of themselves are rarely thought well of by their followers. Moreover, inappropriate dependency in ministry is unhealthy. Some positions taken for granted today are relatively recent, such as the power of the bishop. Other positions with complicated historical development are presented as having simple, uniform, and speedy development, such as the centrality of priesthood. "Sacred traditions" are frequently the constantly repeated views of the theological victors of political history—views that are then read into Scripture and thus given further support and authority. There are some often-repeated, but ill-founded views, that we would do well to forget.

The call to cooperate with others in ministry will be a paschal experience. There are so many pressures against it, it would be easier to abandon the effort. However, collaboration is a way of being Church in a relevant way for the late eighties and early nineties and must be courageously pursued.

Support Systems for Those Who Work Together

Christians who dedicate themselves to team ministry or administration need a high degree of self-confidence and self-esteem. They will need integrity and Christian fortitude. Since conflict will be a part of their lives they must learn to see it as normal, desirable, and offering potential for growth. Since the best any member of a team can hope for is 15 percent rejection—a minister must generally expect more rejection than that—all ministers must be willing to be unloved. No team can be totally harmonious, and so each one must confront differences constructively and know which issues are worth fighting over.

Since collaboration is an intense experience, each member of the team must assure himself or herself, and be assured by others, of channels of support.

The first support for a minister is competence. Those who are responsible need to recruit ministers carefully, give serious attention to placement, and make expectations very clear. The team then gives attention to the educational and experiential background of new candidates for the position in a team. Regular annual evaluations can be means to affirm team members competence or honestly challenge them to be as good as they can be. Regular professional evaluation by teams may eventually spur the hierarchy into professional evaluation.

A second support for team members is good health. This self-responsibility should include nutritional awareness, physical fitness, good use of leisure, stress management, adequate sleep, and guaranteed time away from ministry. Team members can prolong their effectiveness if they take care of their own health and challenge colleagues to do likewise.

A major contribution to good health for the team members is deep and lasting friendships that satisfy human need for intimacy, admittedly attained in different ways for the married, single, or celibate. We all need significant friends with whom we can share our concerns and hopes, be ourselves, and simply enjoy life. The restorative power of friendship can never be laid aside. For married laity, a satisfying sexual life strengthens ministry, and where it is absent the commitment to ministry will quickly disintegrate.

A fourth support for collaborative ministry is found when colleagues legitimate the role of each other. To affirm and celebrate the success of team members and to speak publicly in support of their ministry notably strengthens, gives confidence, and generates a feeling of well-being within the group. Avoiding the dominant male attitudes of contrast and comparison, teams always can be supportive of the variety of their members' charisms.

Role legitimation can be complemented by other forms of team support: letters of appreciation from the pastor, salary increases for notable achievements, public recognition for pastoral services, diocesan acknowledgment of success and dedication, availability of educational scholarships, diocesan awards for outstanding team members. All these forms of team support help to maintain hope, optimism, and motivation.

Ministers in teams also need to get away from their teams from time to time and share with their peers outside their immediate working environment. If a team has a youth minister, he or she requires the support and understanding of other youth ministers. Networking with one's peers gives opportunity to discuss problems, find understanding, and benefit from others' similar experiences.

Cooperation in ministry will increase in the years ahead, and more and more nonclerics will choose ministry as their profession. Parish councils and diocesan boards can prepare by evaluating their employment practices and making sure they reflect a Christian approach to work and the worker. Are salaries and fringe benefits adequate enough to allow a family to live above the poverty level? Are there medical and pension plans, opportunities for advancement, levels of security at least comparable with the clergy's, procedures for times of disagreement and appeal?

Every member of a team must first of all be true to himself or herself before they can do anything for others. Those who wish to participate in Christian ministry by working together with others should assure themselves of a stable prayer life, moral integrity, and spiritual direction, which make them worthy of their task. The group can enrich each one's personal Christian life through shared prayer, shared faith, team liturgy, days of reflection, and revision of life.

Institutionalizing the Vision

Working together in ministry is an excellent contribution to the communion of the Church. As we work together we search for a vision that we do not have at the start. It is an ongoing communal discernment where each one risks himself or herself in sharing with others, and at the same time tries to discover the unique individuality that every member of the team brings to the common undertaking. It will necessitate training (and there is little excuse for not having it), constructive self-analysis (and there is not much of this in our Church), and a careful screening of all who are in visible ministries.

Working together in ministry is a way of living the shared responsibility to which baptism calls us. Collaborative approaches to administration and ministry are parts of a prophetical vision that is wonderful to anticipate and extremely painful to attain. Christianity has an opportunity of becoming a renewed religion but to do so must be willing to change nonessentials. The institution's present commitment to this effort is ambiguous at best. In contrast to the faithful, the institutional Church is a two-thousand-year-old institution that frequently identifies its own absolutes with Christ's. Although some of its officials—lay, religious, and priests—have visionless eyes, others hope and yearn for changes that may still make their religion meaningful to them and relevant to their world. Teams that cooperate are part of that vision, but if it is to last, it must be institutionalized. This is a difficult, delicate, and painful task. However, selecting, synthesizing, articulating, and evaluating the vision is part of collaboration. We get people's commitment by focusing their attention on the vision, inviting their participation in attaining a consensus, and letting them see that their contribution gives life to the group ideal. It is a process of communal commitment to a shared ideal.

Laity involved in common ventures should organize themselves in order to avoid fragmentation of their common hopes. Laity within a diocese do well to establish their own executive committee to parallel the presbyteral council. Through this committee they can strive for just wages that will adequately support their families, fringe benefits such as adequate insurance, pension plans and medical coverage, and appropriate contracts that will give job stability and security.

It is unfortunate that it is necessary for laity to take measures to protect themselves against injustices in Church administration. We all wish it were otherwise but know that in some cases it is not. Collaboration can be more healthily achieved when participants know that a change of pastor will not end their work, or a threatened pastor cannot destroy their team. Dedicated pastors who are men of vision also treat their lay colleagues justly. It is against others that laity need the security of diocesan protection.

Collaboration is also strengthened when there are clear procedures and due process in cases of conflict. The hair-raising stories of sinful terminations of laity and religious at the whim of some authoritarian newcomer—priest or bishop—must come to an end. When participants know they will be treated justly, collaborative ventures can work; otherwise we see laity striving for their private principalities within the established private kingdom of the pastor.

Part of the institutionalizing of collaboration is diocesan control of job descriptions so that team members are not constantly accumulating new assignments. The appointment of a lay diocesan vicar for career lay ministers would also help, provided he or she is well qualified, in constant dialogue with career lay ministers and possibly elected by them. It is clear that collaboration will not work without the transitional support of top officials, especially the bishop. This is difficult when the Vatican is so visibly concerned to stress the role of the hierarchy, when some bishops are so concerned with pleasing the Vatican, and when the new code gives so little support to the laity's role in Church structures. Courageous bishops who are dedicated to the good of their present diocese can do so much to initiate collaborative approaches to administration and ministry. Such bishops will not impose clergy on teams without consultation, nor will they allow excellent religious and laity to leave their diocese in search of a vision of Church. Needless to say, no bishop can expect collaboration in his parishes if he does not establish collaborative approaches to his diocesan administration.

Collaboration challenges us to new models of ministry, new directions for the training of Church personnel, new efforts to maintain a climate that is conducive to working together, constant effort to react to the negative forces in ministry, prudence to develop adequate support systems, and wisdom and foresight to institutionalize the vision.

Critical Issues in Working Together

Sharing Life

Ministers who work together may well have their main life support group outside of the team of which they are members. Moreover, when teams are formed, their purpose is a common ministerial undertaking and not faith sharing. Nevertheless working together within a faith context requires some sharing on the levels of intellect, vision, administration, and faith. Groups will determine their level of sharing depending on their own stage of growth.

To work well together in a local church, each member of the team needs to know himself or herself, the group they are working with, the situation the local church is in, and the agreed goals of the team.

Clearly the team is not intended to carry an overdependent person. Ministry is for a maturing Christian. Nevertheless, by presence and words, members show each other their friendship, professional support, and common vision of faith.

Aids to Group Growth.

Below are a series of forms of faith sharing with appropriate methods and topics for sharing. As the team meets weekly or monthly, they could use one or other of these exercises to enrich their communion. The various aids presented below are not given in a definite, chronological order. When a given practice is to be introduced depends on the intuition and charism of the leaders. However, the aids are given in an order that in general moves with the growth of the group. Deep growth comes with the integrated use of several forms of sharing, not simply a progression through the list. Some offer different ways of viewing a basic form of sharing. To give a detailed explanation of each with its history, advantages, purpose, and results, would need a book in itself. I have limited myself to a point-form presentation.

1. Gospel Sharing

Method:
 Select a leader.
 Begin with prayer.
 Reflect prayerfully and silently, requesting openness to the Holy Spirit.
 The leader selects a reading from Scripture.

Reflect in silence.

Share reflections, questions, and answers.

Bring the sharing to end with prayer. (Leader does this at a time previously agreed upon by group.)

Comments:

This is a simple study of a passage of Scripture.

It is not personally applied and therefore does not threaten.

At the end of such sessions, the leader could gradually lead the group to shared prayer or communication of life on these particular words of Scripture.

2. Group Liturgy

Method:

Prepare liturgy. (At first, let a couple of enthusiasts do it.)

Gradually lead all the group to involvement.

Avoid too much novelty, yet educate the group to new possibilities.

Comments:

From time to time, revise liturgical life.

Do not allow original leadership to remain for long.

Let it be appreciated that all must lead in some dimension of worship.

Make certain liturgy preparations infrequent and brief.

3. Shared Prayer

Method:

Begin with silence.

Pray to the Holy Spirit.

Read Scripture.

Reflect in silence—from which vocalized prayer springs.

Unite oneself to all the sentiments expressed in prayer.

Comments:

We are concerned here with shared spontaneous prayers.

Have a definite leader and an agreed length of time for prayer.

Expect mainly prayers of request at first.

Frequently have a session to revise the quality of shared prayer, check monopolizers, and channel to prayer of praise.

If this is a shared prayer session, maintain it on the level of prayer. Do not drop to shared reflections.

Keep the group open to new members.

Instead of a reading, it is sometimes good to use a few slides that inspire wonder, gratitude, or sorrow.

If the atmosphere is right, even a coal or log fire can lead us to shared prayer as it did some of the mystics.

4. Communication of Life

Method:

Open with prayer followed by silence.

Start with a reading, a news clipping, or by recalling an incident of the day. Anything can serve as a start.

Ask, How do I personally feel about the issue the group is reflecting on?

Communicate feelings to the group.

Do not allow comments, questions, criticism, or advice by others.

Give others opportunities to share feelings.

End when the leader thinks all who wish to speak have spoken.

Comments:

Do not allow any discussion at all in the session or after it.

Give all the time needed.

Maintain the prayerful atmosphere.

Maybe lead into shared prayer at the end.

Possible Themes for a Communication in Life:

Do I feel accepted in this group? Let me explain why I feel as I do.

What kind of prayer is most helpful for me at this time of life?

Who is Jesus for me?

What does friendship mean for me at this time in my life?

How do I experience the love of the Father for me?

5. Shared Faith Experience

Method:

Same as Communication of Life (see #4 above).

Comments:

This should not be approached until the group is reasonably well formed.

If you begin this too soon, the sharing will be superficial, and it will be harder later to challenge people to something deeper.

When shared prayer and communication of life are consistently good, it can be taken as an indication that the group is ready for the deeper shared faith experience.

Possible Topics:

Why am I a Christian?

Where do I see the providence of the Lord in my life?

How do I experience the cross in my life?
What place does a spirit of sacrifice have in my life?
How do I personally experience the Holy Spirit?
What is my image of God?

6. Group Revision of External Life
Method:

Same as Communication of Life (see #4 above), but the sharing is in the form of group examination of some aspect of its external life.

Comments:

The purpose of this is not to be more efficient but to deepen the commitment of each member of the group to being on mission.
Participants will need humility, consideration and appreciation of others, and a general attitude of benevolence.
Issues raised should be explored with delicacy to avoid hurt.

Possible topics:

How does this group relate to the local parish and pastor?
Is our group completely accepted by the people around us? If so, what is lacking in our prophetical witness?
Is this group understructured for sharing or overstructured for spontaneity?

7. Group Ministry Report
Method:

Begin with prayer.
Allow ample time for each person to report in pleasant, easy atmosphere that communicates group interest.
Ask questions after each report.
Listen attentively to answers given by person reporting.
End in prayers of praise for the achievements of the Lord through the group.

Comments:

A lack of interest in the work of individual members does much damage to group life.

8. Self-Disclosure
Method 1:

Same as Communication of Life (see #4 above).

Possible Themes:

What is the image I have of myself?
Do I feel alone? If so, why?

What am I afraid of?

What are the happy moments I remember in life?

How do I feel about the world today?

What do I hope and expect from life?

Method 2:

Use any selection of large photographs, such as those used in catechetics, and spread out about thirty of them.

Begin with prayer and quiet reflection.

Let each person choose three photos that say something about his or her own life and explain this to the group.

Do not allow discussion, criticism, or comment by the group.

Let all who wish choose photos and share their reflections.

Comment:

As group life develops, each one could take six photos—three for oneself and three for the person near him or her and explain why each photo was selected. This can help the group to affirm the good qualities in each other.

9. Group Sharing of Value Judgments or Personal Reactions

Method:

Discuss the moral issues involved, or your affective reactions to a TV program, movie, news event, etc.

Keep reactions in a faith context.

End with prayer.

Comments:

This does not need method or structure; it needs initiative and timeliness.

This is a spontaneous form of sharing and depends on the initiative of members to start it on a suitable occasion.

10. Shared Meditation

Method:

Begin with silence and prayer to the Holy Spirit.

Read from Scripture. Follow with silence.

Have an individual reflect on the passage, sharing his or her reflection with the group in a prayerful atmosphere.

Follow with a reflection by another member who takes the original reflection a further step. Others offer their reflections, each new speaker picking up on the thoughts of the preceding one.

Gradually the discursive aspects of a meditation proceed—the group meditating as a single mind.

Move into affective prayer (which can then become spontaneous and unconnected) after a sufficient time has passed (twenty minutes).

Comments:

This is an excellent form of prayer to bind the group together, enable listening, and encourage real dialogue.

At the beginning, the presence of an external observer is desirable to assess the group's experience.

11. Revision of Internal Life

Method:

Same as Revision of External Life (see #6 above), but this should be introduced much later after the group has developed a strong sense of trust in their life together.

Possible Themes:

How has the quality of our group's prayer life developed?

What is the sense of sin in the group?

Are we committed to each other?

12. Group Planning

Method:

Identify the attainable hopes of the group.

Determine how long it will take the group to attain them.

Establish realistic intermediate stages or secondary ends in working towards the agreed objectives.

Determine who will have responsibility for meeting which objectives and how this is to be done.

Evaluate at the completion of each intermediate stage.

Comments:

This can be more easily approached when the group uses Communication of Life (see #4 above) occasionally to reflect on the members' hopes and ideals.

13. Group Discernment

Method:

Prepare by prayerfully reflecting on the alternatives presented to the group for decision.

Pray for genuine freedom of spirit.

Make a genuine effort to become informed.

Pray and reflect privately on each alternative.

Present to the group reasons for each alternative, plus prayerful reflection and evaluation.

Discuss alternatives.
Seek consensus or vote on alternatives.

Comments:

It is important to maintain a prayerful atmosphere.

The members may go apart for each reflection period, or if time is limited, stay in the same room.

Do not expect the Holy Spirit to keep to our timetables.

In the early stages of group discernment, do not expect answers or complete results.

In time, this becomes a wonderful, ecclesial, and Spirit-filled experience.

14. Group Mutual Correction

Method:

Begin with prayer.

Reflect on the blessings the Lord had given to the group and to each individual in the group.

Each member shares within the group the particular failing he or she would like to see removed from the group's life.

No discussion follows.

Comments:

Reciprocal love is a prerequisite.

The group should only introduce this after they have worked together for at least two years and attained a good depth of group sharing.

It is important to examine motivation beforehand.

Planning for Common Work

A mature team integrates growth in friendship and growth in a common task. Any ministry accomplished by individual members is the common ministry of the team. Together the team discerns direction, plans, sets its standards, facilitates the participation of all, keeps everyone informed, and encourages and supports each other.

Planning in Faith.

The future is open to a variety of possibilities, and many approaches will mold and form our families, Church, and world in the next ten years. However, the very openness of the future is an invitation and a challenge to create a reality that we would experience as satisfying on both an individual and a communal level. The following methodology facilitates planning for the future from a Christian perspective.

The usual method of planning is from the present to the future. This method attempts to look at the present from the future perspective. Thus our concrete planning is more influenced by the created future, and steps are taken from that perspective. This planning process is filled with hope as well as a belief in transformation and change. The following are the stages in the development of this method:

1. The process begins with an analysis of the present situation in which we find ourselves as a family, a community, a Church. How do we see ourselves in regard to our life, mission, effectiveness? How do others see us? What are our strengths and what are the areas that need further development? When the present reality is adequately identified, we leave it aside for a time.

2. The creation of a desirable future is perhaps the most challenging aspect of this methodology because it calls forth the potential and the vision that is often stifled within persons and groups. Living in the future, with the problems and realities of the present blotted out, the participants create an ideal image of their family, community, or Church. All aspects of life and sharing are considered. In this phase, the ideal of the group is presumed to be a reality.

3. The previous two steps lead to a necessary confrontation of the ideal hoped for with the present reality as we have described it. The comparison challenges participants to identify the areas that need to be changed in order for the ideal to be realized. As persons and as a group, the participants see areas of needed healing and transformation. This reflective stage deepens insights and commitment, and clarifies obstacles and potentials.

4. The planning stage begins with the ideal image or goal of the group. This long-term goal is then embodied in a series of objectives.

5. However, more than objectives is needed. The group also plans the appropriate action items, the steps that will be taken in order to make the ideal a reality within a given period of time. The ideal is not handed over to a few to work out and achieve, but responsibilities are specified for each member of the group. The following questions are answered at each stage of planning: What is to be done? Who is to do it? When is it to be done? Where is it to be done? How?

Why? The result is a workable plan which is the creation of the participants.

There are many advantages in using this method. It integrates psychological and spiritual realities, sociological and faith dimensions of life. It involves the participants on a level of sharing and dialogue so that the very qualities that are needed to make the ideal a reality are being exercised and developed in the process. The method is a Christian, hope-filled one. Furthermore, the method integrates content, sharing, reflection; the process itself educates. Prayer and discernment, more than technique, are the backbone of the process. In a practical way, the problems of the present do not bog us down. The future can be different, if we want it to be.

How long is needed for a group to use this method effectively? Various groups can use this form of planning—parishes, families, religious communities, neighborhood and faith sharing groups, priests, service groups, parish councils. The desirable length of time varies with each group. A full weekend (Friday through Sunday) is good. However, fine results are seen in shorter periods depending on the group. A longer time (the evenings of a week or two) gives the opportunity to explore in depth and create deeper bonds on the level of community experience.

The key to effectiveness is ongoing evaluation, and this is built into the planning. This planning is an exciting, relaxed, and practical approach to help us move creatively and effectively into the future we desire. As Christians, can we do anything less that transform our lives and communities into a living witness to gospel values?

Sharing Responsibilities for Ministry.

As a team matures, the various works the individual members accomplish become more and more the ministry of the whole team. Each member takes an interest in all the tasks of the group. While a team leaves its specialists to oversee their own areas of responsibilities, the team should create opportunities to manifest their interest in the specialized ministries achieved by their colleagues. An annual schedule should identify the times when each ministerial specialist will have opportunity to report on his or her work. Each one should also keep team members updated on their work through memos or newsletters. Moreover, frequently there are projects in which the whole team can share at different levels and should do so. While one member of a team may be responsible for a particular project, others could be actively involved, consulted, or at least informed.

Working Together to Improve Parish Participation.

Fr. Philip Murnion ("Eight Ways to Improve Parish Participation," *Today's Parish,* March 1983, 19–21) suggests eight ways to improve parish participation: listen, put first things first, share and clarify responsibilities, equip people adequately, respect other people's talents and gifts, provide a context of reflection and prayer, ensure adequate support, and ensure a climate of equality.

Evaluations

Anyone working with others in the Church today needs to foster responsible evaluation of themselves and of all members of the team. This goes against the tide of irresponsible nonevaluation in the churches and therefore requires spiritual courage, prayer, ascetical commitment, and a spirit of nonaggressiveness.

If the team is collaborative and mature, then supervision will be welcome and mutual, and evaluation will be constructive feedback.

Self-Evaluation of My Ability to Work With Others

	Yes	No	Comments	Recommended Action
1. Am I professional about my work?				
2. Do I keep up to date?				
3. Do I read and study regularly?				
4. Do I take time for relaxation?				

Self-Evaluation of My Ability to Work With Others (continued)

	Yes	No	Comments	Recommended Action
5. Is my prayer life developing?				
6. Have I appropriate support systems?				
7. Am I respected by my peers?				
8. Do I like the people I work with?				
9. Do we have a similar understanding of Church and ministry?				
10. Do colleagues have confidence in me?				
11. Can I be trusted to complete my projects on schedule?				

Self-Evaluation of My Ability to Work With Others (continued)

	Yes	No	Comments	Recommended Action
12. Do I contribute significantly to this local church?				
13. Do I show interest in my colleagues' work?				
14. Do I let them have other interests besides our common work?				
15. Do I seek their views and advice?				
16. Do they seek my input?				
17. Do I share deeply with the team?				
18. Has my role increased in this team?				

Self-Evaluation of My Ability to Work With Others (continued)

	Yes	No	Comments	Recommended Action
19. Do they feel free to give me feedback on my work?				
20. Do I do offer feedback to the team?				
21. Can I deal with conflict?				
22. Do we pray together?				
23. Have we formulated our mission statement?				

Community Evaluation of Its Ministers

Whatever your local church community—a parish, neighborhood, school, social service agency, youth gathering, retreat center, or so on—once a year you should give the people you minister to the opportunity to evaluate your services. Their evaluating you can also give them an opportunity for a little self-evaluation.

We your ministers take the occasion of this annual evaluation to thank you for the opportunity of serving you. It is truly a blessing for which we are grateful. We wish to serve you well, meet your expectations of us, and make our local church a community you are happy to belong to and find enriching in your lives.

Please answer the following questions to aid us in our annual assessment and planning.

	Yes	No	Don't Know	Comments
1. Do the staff work well together?				
2. Are you aware of conflict or bad spirit in the staff?				
3. Do they portray a sense of unity?				
4. Is the local church growing as a result of their services?				
5. Have you participated in any of the programs they have sponsored?				
6. Are you satisfied with the performance of their responsibilities? a. Pastor? b. Associate Pastor? c. Pastoral Minister? d. Director of Education? e. Youth Minister? f. Support staff? g. Other?				

	Yes	No	Don't Know	Comments
7. Are the staff up to date in their own areas of competence?				
8. Do the staff show a spirit of cooperation with the bishop and diocesan officers?				
9. Are adequate programs conducted in the local church?				
10. Do you feel a sense of ownership for the parish?				
11. Are you satisfied with the church's (parish council's) treatment of the staff?				
12. Do the staff have ability to involve people in their programs?				
13. If everyone in the parish contributed as much financial support as you do, would all these services be financed?				

I. List the events (other than Sunday Liturgy) that you have attended this year.

II. If you do not attend local church events, please indicate briefly why.

III. List those services you would like to see offered by the staff.

IV. What could they do that they are not doing?

V. What could you do that you are not doing?

Peer Evaluation

Answer the following questions yourself, and let all members of the team answer them for you. Invite the rest of the staff to meet without you and share their evaluations of you, discuss them, refocus them if necessary, and present their report and recommendations to you orally or in writing. If you have responsibilities to lead larger groups of the local church, invite staff to be present to evaluate your public performance.

1. Vision of Church

	Yes	No	Don't Know
a. Does this minister have an up-to-date vision of Church?			
b. Is the vision nourished by study, reflection, and sharing?			
c. Is this member's vision comparable to the rest of the team's?			
d. Is this member's ecclesiology faithful to the vision of the universal Church?			
e. Is this colleague characterized by a sense of Church?			

Please add your comments.

Feel free to specify your areas of concern.

2. Sense of Ministry

	Yes	No	Don't Know
a. Does this staff member treat his or her job as a ministry?			
b. Does this staff member give clear signs of a sense of call?			
c. Is this colleague selfless in his or her service of others?			
d. Does this member embody Christian discipleship?			
e. Can this member integrate the trials of ministry into his or her vocational commitment?			

Please add your comments

Feel free to specify areas of concern.

3. Professional Competence	Yes	No	Don't Know
a. Has this person fulfilled the responsibilities of the job for which he or she was hired?			
b. Is this member competent, responsible, and able to lead in the specific area of his or her ministry?			
c. If you were hiring for this position now, would you hire this member?			
d. Are you aware of this person's ongoing efforts to keep up-to-date professionally?			
e. Can this person make decisions?			

Please add your comments.

Feel free to specify areas of concern.

4. Relationships

	Yes	No	Don't Know
a. Can this colleague work well with others?			
b. Does he or she relate well with other members of the staff?			
c. Is this person at ease with others?			
d. Does this member have good and lasting friendships?			
e. If married, is the member's family life a model for others?			
f. Can this member work with a team?			

Please add your comments.

Feel free to specify areas of concern.

5. Working with Members of the Church Community

	Yes	No	Don't Know
a. Can this person relate well to people from varied walks of life and levels of commitment?			
b. Is this person at ease when leading groups?			
c. Does the community see this person as a man or woman of stature and responsibility?			
d. Is this person accepted as a pastoral leader?			
e. Can this person recruit volunteers and inspire them with enthusiasm for their shared ministry?			
f. Can this member delegate?			

Please add your comments.

Feel free to specify areas of concern.

6. *Spiritual Growth*	Yes	No	Don't Know
a. Is this person's ministry supported by quality Christian life?			
b. Do people acknowledge this minister as a person who embodies what the Church proclaims?			
c. Would you consider this colleague a person of prayer?			
d. Does this staff member respond with Christian attitudes to the common problems in ministry?			
e. Is this staff member a person of the Church?			

Please add your comments.

Feel free to specify areas of concern.

7. Christian Witness

	Yes	No	Don't Know

a. Is this person's life prophetically challenging?
b. Is this member a Christian example that others should follow?
c. Does this person do a fair day's work?
d. Is this staff member a generous servant leader?
e. Does this person embody the Church's call to proclaim peace, justice, and concern for the poor?

Please add your comments.

Feel free to specify areas of concern.

8. Conclusions

	Yes	No	Don't Know

a. Are there notable achievements in this person's ministry this year that ought to receive public recognition?
b. Is there any negative issue in this person's ministry that, if it continued, would jeopardize the stability of his or her job?

Topics for Reflection and Discussion

Is Your Team a Caring Group?

Do you individually contribute to the community quality of your team, and do you receive care and support from other team members? Check the following signs of care in a group that works together in ministry.

	Show to Others	Receive It
Politeness		
Benevolence		
Acceptance as significant member		
Empathy		
Respect		
Trust		
Shared responsibility		
Support for new members		
Appreciation		
Healthy give and take of adults		

Questions for Group Sharing

1. How can lay ministers be directly involved in decision making?
2. How can you get many people involved and still get something done?
3. Who are the significant ministers in your life and why?
4. What are the specific gifts that women bring to ministry?
5. How do priests, religious, and laity mutually help each other in their team experience of ministry?
6. Is there an essential difference between the ministry of clergy and nonclergy? If so, what is it?
7. How can lay ministers gain acceptance by the people, especially when they break role stereotypes for ministry?
8. List requirements that every minister—priest, religious, or lay—ought to meet to retain his or her professional standing?
9. What could your parish do to create a climate for the development of lay ministry?

10. Since lay ministers are generally paid poorly, give some practical suggestions to help the lay minister increase his or her salary base.

Some Concerns about Working Together Expressed by Lay Ministers

If there is a disagreement, the male clergy tends to downgrade the input of the laity or to resort to "authority" rather than open discussion. As a woman I often experience pastors who are unwilling to make use of and/or trust information coming from my office, simply because a lay, married woman is head of it.

•

Team ministry is frustrating only when I fail to acknowledge that all obstacles are opportunities to experience growth!

•

Trouble arises with lack of human understanding of one another. Clear-cut expectations are needed; sometimes "turf" defense gets in the way. A group needs to mature as a group and needs to be careful of "ganging up" on one member.

•

I find it satisfying to work with people, but not with the staff, which has increasingly become more efficient and business oriented. At times decisions are made, and the director changes them without notice—just whim. We don't discuss who makes what decisions and why.

•

There is still sexual bias, exclusive language, and antiquated thinking regarding laity, especially women. Men are in control, whereas women give up control and complain about it.

Selected Reading

Doohan, Leonard, ed. *John Paul II and the Laity*. New York: Human Development Books, 1984.

Finn, Virginia S. *Pilgrim in the Parish: A Spirituality for Lay Ministers*. New York: Paulist Press, 1986.

Geaney, Dennis. *Full Church, Empty Rectory: Training Lay Ministers for Parishes Without Priests.* Notre Dame, IN: Fides/Claretian, 1980.

Southard, Samuel. *Comprehensive Pastoral Care: Enabling the Laity to Share in Pastoral Ministry.* Valley Forge, PA: Judson, 1975.

U.S. Bishops' Committee on the Laity. *Growing Together: Conference on Shared Ministry.* Washington, DC: National Catholic Conference of Bishops, 1980.

Additional Reading

Doohan, Leonard. *The Laity: A Bibliography.* Wilmington, DE: Michael Glazier, Inc., 1987. See sections 12, 14, 17, 22, 24, 25.

Chapter 4

MINISTERING IN CHURCH STRUCTURES

Lay Ministers Speak About Ministering in Church Structures

Reflections

Introduction
Working for the Institutional Church
An Opportunity for Growth
Sharing in the Lord's Ministry
Participation in Christ's Suffering Servanthood
Mutual Support of Lay Professionals
Aids to Stability in Ministry

Critical Issues When Ministering in Church Structures

Increasing Job Stability
Some Useful Diocesan Experiences
Policy Changes in the Local Church to Protect Lay Ministers

Topics for Reflection and Discussion

Looking after Yourself as a Minister
Questions for Group Sharing

Some Concerns about Ministering in Church Structures Expressed by Lay Ministers

Selected Reading

Lay Ministers Speak About Ministering in Church Structures

There is a growing understanding of who and what is Church. Experiences of parish councils have helped. However, so much of the structure is dependent on the attitude of the pastor.

•

Ecclesiastical structures enhance my ministry. Yes, the structures provide guidelines, direction, supports that are conducive to collaboration in ministry.

•

Last year, due to priest shortage, I served as associate pastor of the parish and was seen as such by the parish but not by the diocese.

•

The director of the office is helpful in giving me assistance when I need it, and he gives me much freedom and trust in developing areas that I am interested in.

•

The institution I work in is trying very hard to herald the Word, serve others, and call others to service.

•

The warmth and openness of this parish helps to support me so that I can minister better. Our distance from the chancery also helps!

Reflections

Introduction

There are 825 million Catholics throughout the world. The United States is divided into 185 dioceses and 19,313 parishes. Lay contribution to local church life is increasing annually, and there are now more paid laity in parish administrative positions than religious—in fact 57 percent. When volunteers are added, laity total 83 percent of all the parish leadership outside of the pastor's. Over 64 percent of all United States' parishes now involve intervocational leadership teams of clergy, religious, and laity, and this figure is increasing annually. In 10 percent of our parishes laity are the key administrators.

The lay minister is a special blessing to our generation, and like New Testament times the Church's stability, growth, and development depend on the critical contributions of laity. Unfortunately, career lay ministers have not been welcomed or appreciated as they ought to have been. Many of those who were first to enter ministry around the time of Vatican II have been increasingly burdened with responsibilities, and the burned-out have left ministry, unlikely to return. The average length of time spent in parish-affiliated lay ministries is three years, the first year being the most critical.

We have invested most of our money in Catholic schools, many of which closed after the drop in enrollment in the sixties and seventies. Some parishes have merged their schools, and others only maintain enrollment by increasing the numbers of non-Catholics or non-Christians. Although some may wish to continue our school ministry, we must also give careful attention to the extensive services of other lay ministers and strengthen their positions of responsibility in our local churches. We might compare how many teachers we hire in parishes for 100–200 students with budget, space, and personnel allocation to the many needs of other parish pastoral ministries.

Parish councils can assure their parishes of top lay leadership and be particularly protective of their personnel in these critical times of transition. Unfortunately, some parish councils have approved unjust wages for their lay ministers, been miserly in fringe benefits, and short-sighted in budget allocation to the ministry programs of their parishes. Council members who have lacked a vision of Church and remain blind to future developments have sometimes produced battered ministers, forced to work with little and for little, and who eventually can do nothing but leave.

The major expression of Church life today is local. For better or worse, the future of our universal Church depends on the vision and vitality of our local churches. All the more reason for stressing the importance of the local lay ministers, treating them with respect and dignity, recompensing them justly, and assuring them of stability. In coming decades many United States Catholics will meet the institutional Church in the lay minister; in fact, he or she will be the administrational Church for ever increasing numbers of the faithful who will rarely see a bishop, a priest, or a religious.

Fortunately the future looks good. There is no shortage of qualified vocations in the Churches as increasing numbers of well-educated and well-trained laity sacrifice comfort, better salaries, advancement opportunities, long-term security, and accept the vocation to ministry. These laity become the clearest signs of evangelical life in the Church. They live simple and poor lives, trusting in the providence of the Lord who called them. They are a prophetical challenge to a materialistic world, and they dedicate themselves to local churches that frequently treat them with disdain or worse still ignore them.

This chapter deals with the professional lay minister working within a church structure. While this local structure is most frequently the parish, it could also be the diocesan administration, or a social service agency, or education where lay ministers dedicate themselves to Church-related schools for ministerial purposes. Workers in regional, national, or international spiritual movements that are Church related and under the authority of Church management would also be included, as well as the many diocesan lay-guided programs founded to give retreats, aid the needy, care for the oppressed, and visit the sick or imprisoned. The chapter refers to anyone whose life and work are a ministry and who receive payment from Church structures for the services they perform.

Working for the Institutional Church

Some highly structured organizations have reputations of changing slowly and reluctantly. Universities are examples of hierarchically governed institutions that have changed very little over the decades, and even though they utilize many committees for their projects, they remain autocratically governed. They are frequently characterized by polarization between administration and faculty, and considerable anger. Parish and diocesan structures are similarly reluctant to change, and the permanence of hierarchical structures and autocratic government is far more common than is their absence. Anyone who dedicates himself or herself to work within these structures must do so with a mature awareness of what they are getting into. At the same time, entry-level personnel in professional ministry need to realize that there are other professions and organizations that are little different than the Church in their structures and styles of government.

Service to the institutional Church is a generous vocational commitment. Through baptism we are all members of the Church we love, and anyone may feel called to serve other believers in the institutional Church irrespective of state in life. To describe a layperson in such service as a "paraclerical" and the increased numbers of laity entering such service as "the clericalization of laity" is unwarranted. In fact, such terminology betrays a lack of appreciation of history and theology and seems to be used as a contemporary put-down of laity who choose such dedication. All members of the Church have rights to serve in this way, and the faithful should be grateful rather than introduce a label whose only purpose is to make it look as if this choice in life is unsuitable or inappropriate for laity. Without career lay ecclesial ministers the contemporary Church could not continue its current levels of service. Laity are in fact the largest ministerial group in the Church.

The first important step in the hiring of a layperson as an ecclesial minister in the local church is to prepare the congregation to appreciate, want, and later accept, a lay minister. This means informing them of parish needs that have been previously generated from the community and showing how a layperson can fulfill these needs. If the parish has not previously hired a layperson, the staff could show what the national trends are and how well laity have performed in our growing Church. I find that many hirings of laity are done by the pastor or parish staff, forgetting that without involvement, the congregation will show no ownership of the new venture.

The hiring process cannot be motivated by the pursuit of cheap labor, nor can the suggestion to search for a sister whose salary would be even smaller be dignified with religious motives. Every ecclesial minister has the potential of major influence on parish life, and each new hiring is a very serious undertaking.

Some diocesan offices act as a clearing house for all hirings, where this is not done the parish should give candidates a job description that everyone agrees to, an outline of current staff responsibilities and lines of accountability, a brief history of the parish and its social and religious analysis, the staff's mission statement, the parish's goals and objectives, the diocese's goals and objectives, the diocese's pastoral plan, and indications of salary and fringe benefits. It can also be particularly helpful to speak about the parish's approach to current "touchy issues," such as nonordained preaching or the roles of women. Since touchy issues are the ones that later can cause so much trouble, it is important to openly discuss them.

Applicants should send a résumé of their education, training, and previous positions held, letters of reference preferably from various vocations, telephone numbers of referees who could be contacted for more detailed information, and a written statement on the candidate's personal theology of Church and of ministry.

A committee can be made up of present staff, parish council members, parishioners, a diocesan staff representative, and a neighboring parish's minister who fulfills responsibilities similar to those for which the candidate is applying. The composition of the committee shows the parish's vision of Church, its awareness of the need of unity with the diocese, and its spirit of mutual support of nearby parishes.

This committee, having scaled down the applicants to two or three, should invite them to the parish for interviews with the committee. It is advisable that the applicant be present for the church's weekend services so that he or she can see the staff in action and be available after Mass to meet parishioners. The visit gives the applicant an opportunity to meet the staff and parishioners, to review the budget, and to see the office setup. Small issues such as offices can convey the hierarchy within the staff. Differences in furniture, equipment, and even room size can be very informative to an attentive interviewee.

This time-consuming and expensive interview process gives the staff chance to make clear their expectations as to responsibilities and lifestyle, and also gives the staff the opportunity of presenting the potential new member to the parish community thereby involving them in the hiring decision.

The staff will know before the interview how well qualified the person is. Consequently that is not the purpose of the on-site interview. Rather the important purpose of the visit is to clarify expectations. These include responsibilities, authority, levels of team collaboration, forms of faith sharing within the team, process of accountability, intentions for ongoing education, and personal Christian lifestyle. It gives everyone the chance to get a feel for each other and whether they would be comfortable working together.

After the interviews, the committee gathers input from all involved and after discussion and prayer makes a choice. Candidates who are not chosen should receive a letter of appreciation worthy of the Christian vision of the parish.

An Opportunity for Growth

To be an ecclesial minister is not so much an occasion for doing what you want to do, but rather an opportunity to be who you want to be. Response to this call results in the redirection of life, it is an experience that will have influence upon one's own personality and one's family's too.

Like all vocations, to be an ecclesial minister means responding to a call conscious of having the qualities needed. The minister needs theological and pastoral knowledge, educational skill, and commitment. He or she will also need administrative skills for the ministry: budget management, marketing techniques for programs, human resource management of volunteers, and the vision and skills of collaborative management. The minister should also demonstrate mature spiritual formation.

Ministers can be in control of life and cannot allow the demands of ministry to control them. Consequently, before arriving at a new church the minister would do well to have established his or her priorities, allocated time for prayer and study, and established guarantees for time away from ministry, at home with family or friends.

First-year ministers appropriately keep a time log of their activities. If they were among the lucky 41 percent who receive a job description, they will probably need to rewrite if after the first year. The time log will help reformulate the job description, assess priorities, plan for the future, and reallocate time if necessary. Any of the diaries produced by time management firms would be useful.

The principle responsibility of ecclesial ministers is to be involved in the Lord's business. Through the prime focus of evangelization they daily bring the Church to birth anew. Ministers can expect that about 80 percent of their time will be used for administration, but they need to maintain the prime focus on spirituality and pastoral response to the people's needs. They should direct all administration to this purpose.

Well-organized meetings can help individuals grow professionally and the team to grow in mutual appreciation. However, a common mistake among inexperienced staffs is to have long rambling meetings for which some participants come unprepared. When parish activities are in the evening, meetings during the day tend to become open-ended. It is preferable to keep a schedule and to come prepared to discuss topics previously agreed on in the announced agenda. Meetings should end on time and the conclusions be clearly summarized with each staff member's responsibilities identified. When ministers keep meetings within schedule, extra time can be used for study, reflection, prayer, and other involvement that can utilize ministers' gifts in outreach to others.

First-year ministers need clarity regarding their role and clearly delineated lines of accountability. To whom are you accountable? for what? under what criteria will you be evaluated? It is important, especially in the first year, to discuss the evaluation process with the evaluator as early as convenient.

A new minister can quickly size up the staff and join their approach to issues, including their negative, critical, and sometimes time-wasting attitudes. But the minister who picks their positive approaches and commitment, adds to their vision and nourishes them with sharing. Each minister can be a nurturing, strengthening, hope-filled influence to colleagues on the staff. Be calm, positive, and optimistic about your contribution to the team. New members will need patience, giving time to let others accept them once they have witnessed the new minister's competence.

Ministers are called to fulfill many tasks and arrange many projects. But they are pastoral leaders before all else. If one becomes a project director, it is unlikely that someone with a strong vocational commitment will find it satisfying. Ministers should not accept a reduced ideal of their calling. Otherwise their ministry soon becomes a job complacently accomplished.

To give life to others, as is the minister's calling, is nourishing and rewarding, and irrespective of age the minister becomes a person of stature in the local church. However, this rewarding situation requires vigilance. Some lay ministers have become replacements of dominant clerics that they had so frequently criticized. Ministers need to take care to maintain a spirituality that will keep their lives and generosity in close linkage with the truth of their servant calling.

Lay ministry is an opportunity for personal growth. Christians grow in commitment during the exercise of the major responsibilities of each day. For the lay minister, this is the loving dedication and persevering service to their local church, its people, its problems, and its structure.

Sharing in the Lord's Ministry

Increasing numbers of laity dedicating themselves to ministry are finding vocational fulfillment and the rewards of their service. Their gifts and leadership ability are appreciated by the communities they serve, and many of them are blessed with the opportunity to work with a visionary and collaborative pastor and benefit from his years of pastoral experience. Many parish teams are models for the rest of the diocese. Collaborative teams are no longer an experimental stage in parish organization but have become one of the choices that ministers—including priests and bishops—must explicitly accept or reject.

Around the country career lay ministers manifest enthusiasm for their vocation and portray an attractive form of dedication that increasing numbers wish to pursue. Anyone who has attended regional gatherings of career lay ministers has seen the joy, satisfaction, and spiritual enrichment that accompanies their service.

Some laity begin their career of service in volunteer ministry. By financing their own ministry with their own or their spouse's regular job they avoid many difficulties that face the full-time career lay minister. Some dioceses have excellent ministry training programs for volunteer ministry that give individuals a taste of the joy of serving others and provide a pool from which full-time career lay ministers emerge. The "Tempus" program of the Diocese of Great Falls-Billings and the Lay Ministry Training Program in Tulsa are very fine examples of diocesan efforts to develop lay ministry.

Some dioceses are able to give major support to career lay ministers through programs of education and formation offered through local universities, colleges, or renewal centers. Examples are the Kino Institute in Phoenix or University College of Creighton University.

Sometimes laity who feel called to serve the Church finance their own training in centers outside of their own diocese, preparing themselves for a future they see but their diocesan administration does not.

Selection of full-time career lay ministers is a task that in some dioceses is headed by the centralized diocesan personnel who act as a clearing house for needs and applicants. This procedure standardizes job responsibilities and lets the new hiring feel a part of the particular diocesan church. The descriptions distributed by the archdiocese of Milwaukee are excellent.

Some larger dioceses have shown national leadership in the policies established and personnel guidelines provided to their career lay ministers. The Archdiocese of St. Paul and Minneapolis is an outstanding example of this approach to career ministers, and their extensive work has clearly borne fruit in the sense of dedication to the diocese that hundreds of ministers show.

When a diocese welcomes new ministers, assists in their ongoing training, and makes them feel part of the ministering Church, then an exciting image of Church emerges that gives life and reinforces commitment.

Participation in Christ's Suffering Servanthood

The positive experience of ministry that many laity enjoy is not shared by all career lay ministers. Some lay ministers' lives are difficult, their schedule plays havoc with their personal lives, the daily demands placed on them swallow up their real aims, and their profession is not adequately established to generate the respect and appreciation it deserves. Unemployment is humiliating, but some kinds of employment are too, and as ministers see their college-years friends advance and gain respect, some find their own position humiliating, especially when a man or a woman is treated like a factotum, constantly assigned busywork, and uninvolved in serious planning for the future direction of the Church. This humiliation of lay ministers intensifies when there is no diocesan recognition of their work, no ability to organize as a professional body, no due process for the resolution of serious disagreements, and no adequate scale for salaries and benefits.

Sometimes the level of conformity demanded of the lay minister to the pastor's directives is too much to allow any serious professional input and too restrictive to facilitate Christian growth. Local church structures that thwart the minister's professional and Christian growth leave him or her with a sense of powerlessness in ministry. Moreover, since a person attached to power will inevitably want more, the lay minister may find it easier to change to another church. Those who feel they live beneath a funnel into which new tasks, responsibilities, and directive are placed in ever increasing quantities are forced either to take a stand or to leave.

Confrontation should be "carefrontation" for Christians (Charles Keating, *The Leadership Book* [New York: Paulist Press, 1978], 66). However, this is infrequently the case. Local church structures tend to live based on a series of convictions regarding "self-evident truths," such as the authority of bishop and priest, the inalienable rights of the hierarchy, the canonical requirements of clerical orders for important positions and services in the Church, and so on! These are some among a series of very difficult theological issues that need further research and new interpretation. However, the local lay minister can rarely challenge these positions without being labeled unorthodox, which is one of the system's forms of self-preservation. When confrontation develops, recourse to one of the so-called truths of the faith becomes a form of manipulation that leaves the problems unresolved and the lay minister helpless. Even collaborative groups often work under the possible veto power of a local pastor.

The granting of contracts for lay ministers is increasing, but more needs to be done. It is totally unacceptable, unchristian, and unjust that a layperson's ministry is threatened every time a pastor changes. If the new pastor does not want to retain a lay minister, or to work with a team, or to maintain the work and development of years, he can end it all. This is simply sinful, and dioceses dedicated to justice will be creative in resolving these situations. The bishop or his personnel board should consult the parish ministers before any new assignment, especially when the lay minister may have worked longer in the parish than any priest has.

One of the trials of many lay ministers is the ever meager budget for their department. United States Catholicism has invested heavily in real estate that has now become a weight around our necks, limiting our ability to use people's generous offerings in programs and services that lead to growth. Almost every diocese has some empty building that is hardly used and yet is still being paid for. Another enormous drain on the people's generosity is the cost of seminary training, payments for priests who have been asked to leave the diocese, and expenses for retired priests where parishes and dioceses were shortsighted in not establishing pension plans. Such dioceses need long-term financial planning to rectify current inequities and prepare for adequate future financing of new needs.

Lay ministers can be oppressed by the institutionalized Church's slow transition to a new concept of ministry. They can suffer on several levels, suffering that has led many to deepen their spiritual lives through these experiences and become more apostolically worthy. Others, however, have become hardened, bitter, and unable to pray under the burdens of their calling. The principal painful situations they face are created by the structures and not by the ill will of individuals. However, Christians interested in assuring the continuance of well-qualified lay ministers will work to remove injustice and attain a greater recognition of the quality of ministry that these key laity provide.

Mutual Support of Lay Professionals

The first level of mutual support for lay professionals is their own local team, where they expect to find nourishment and refreshment. A monthly meeting in the form of a half-day retreat for reflection and spiritual enrichment can strengthen the relationship and provide opportunity to reassess the direction of the team's life and work. Sometimes there are "good reasons" presented for omitting weekly or monthly meetings, but a half day's recollection, sometimes with an outside observer-consultant, may surface the real problems and potential of the team. A short time away can give the local team time to dream together and then build on members' hopes by using their vision and gifts to channel the team's energy.

Lay professionals, working within a local church sometimes receive support from the diocesan offices. Sometimes well-known, internal problems lead local lay ministers to disregard the services of diocesan offices. The lay ministers then suffer the loss of the challenge and direction diocesan offices can provide. They also experience a dimishment of their sense of diocesan Church. Diocesan offices can examine themselves to see what services they offer to the lay ministers. Do they bring the diocese's lay ministers together, represent them before the bishop, provide ongoing education? Do they have a due process in place for local disagreements, or does one of them act as arbitrator in time of dispute? Even though jobs and salaries may be arranged at the parish level, do diocesan officers check to make sure salaries and benefits are just? Have they established diocese wide policies? Have they clarified the vocational images of the various ministries within the diocesan Church?

Lay ministers can also have a diocesewide lay senate or assembly of their own along the lines of the priests' senate and sisters' senate.

They can elect an executive committee of their peers to act as a lay council for dialogue with the bishop and chancellor. I can see no reason why they may not petition the appointment, after consultation, of a lay diocesan vicar for career lay ministers. Through these simple structures of senate, council, and vicar, the lay ministers can work calmly and pleasantly towards goals that are necessary for their dignity, support, professional growth, spiritual nourishment, and stability.

As time goes on, what is already the case with many individuals will become more common, namely that the major groups of trained experts in theology, pastoral practice, counseling, and parish services will be laity. Channels need to be set up, goals anticipated, and noncompetitive dialogic structures established to guide the bishop and diocese in a nonthreatening way.

No lay minister should be on his or her own but should always have peer support in the region even if it implies substantial travel. Our Church has experience of the problems associated with leaving a priest or a religious on their own without neighborhood peer support, and we can avoid this problem for laity. Lay ministers, especially in their early years, benefit from a mentor who can support, advise, encourage, and challenge. It is rarely a big problem to find one, and predecessors have learned how to live in and with the system and grow in the process.

A form of mutual support that lay ministers can provide for each other is setting standards of qualifications, ongoing certification, and evaluation by peers. This sort of professional control is best when done internally to the group, thus showing the group's own concern for standards rather than seeing them as a threat coming from outside the group.

At present there are few national or international standards or guidelines. As far as the international Church at the Vatican is concerned, there are no formal, universally accepted lay ministries other than lector and acolyte. Major Church authorities have no recognizable bodies to deal with, no fixed ministries. This limits the long-term impact of these lay ministers internal to the Church they sacrificingly serve. Lay ministers would do well to set up national and international organizations in dialogue with Church authorities to offer opinion, and work towards accepted goals.

Aids to Stability in Ministry

A great institution is characterized by caring not only for others but especially for its own employees. After years of study on justice and the economy, we know we cannot proclaim justice while living unjustly, and so we challenge ourselves to caringly analyze our Church system to determine what in the system fosters injustice.

Lay ministers should be assured of information regarding Church matters. Prudence may call for some material to be withheld on occasions, but constant secrecy over issues of public concern is a vice of the international Church that is sometimes contagious. Ministers need to know they have been trusted and kept informed.

Each local church needs structures and procedures that guarantee fairness. Such procedures are easy to set up, and examples are readily available in dioceses with caring bishops. To know one will receive protection, a fair hearing, and a just resolution of disputes goes a long way to create a sense of being wanted and respected in a diocese.

Although the 1985 code reduces laity to merely consultative votes, some local dioceses are setting up procedures that will directly involve lay ministers in decision making at the parish and diocesan levels. To ignore a lay minister of fifteen years experience and ministerial success while accepting input from a newly ordained, inexperienced priest is ludicrous. To confirm that this is Canon Law does not decrease the element of magic or divination.

Visibility and respect are basic aids to stability. It is amazing how often diocesan newspapers repeat the same life history of a cleric as he receives new assignments on a regular basis, whereas lay ministers who have dedicated years of their lives to the same diocese are seldom, if ever, mentioned. Occasions to give them visibility and public acknowledgment are easy to find if one wishes to do so.

At the diocesan level lay ministers can be appointed to important boards (generally diocesan staff are but not local parish ministers). They can be invited to major diocesan celebrations (clergy always are). They can be consulted by the bishop in areas where they have competence. It is also appropriate to schedule diocesan days of lay ministry vocations.

At the parish level, some pastors do an excellent job of public acclaim of their lay ministers, but others never seem to entertain the idea. It takes little effort to recognize the anniversary of lay minister appointments; put on a parish celebration after five or ten years of service; give them major liturgical roles in the ceremony appointing volunteers to the ministry they oversee; single them out for recognition after special successes; remind the bishop when he needs to make a diocesan acknowledgment of their services.

Freedom of opinion is a natural right of everyone. A common position of the Church on doctrinal issues and of a local diocese or parish on a broad range of issues is desirable. However, many priests have always exerted their rights to differ even from diocesan vision and policy, a practice that has sometimes led to scandal. Plenty of occasions still exist for legitimate differences of opinion in theological and pastoral issues and lay ministers' opinions should be respected. Otherwise stress increases and interferes with ministry.

Love proves itself in justice, and justice is shown by respect of others. This vision and commitment can be concretely seen in the way a church handles the contract of a lay minister. The contract is like a covenant between the local church and the minister. The signing can be solemnized, and many parishes have excellent written forms of commitment of lay ministers. The contract should also be worthy of the Church. It is not fair when a career lay minister of several years' service still receives an annually renewed contract. In such circumstances, a parish can terminate a minister simply by not renewing a contract. The possibility of passive termination erodes the mutual commitment there ought to be between the minister and the local community. Salaries can be determined by what similar levels of education and skills would earn for other jobs in the neighborhood. Fringe benefits can be calculated in the same way. The contract also includes a commitment to the diocese and a diocesan commitment to the minister. While a trial period with graded levels of commitment is necessary, there should eventually be some indication of stability. If the bishop wants the right to impose an awkward pastor on a parish where there has previously been a collaborative priestly leader, then the bishop must accept the employment and financial obligations of the lay minister whom the newcomer could displace.

Lay ministry offers very few opportunities for advancement. This problem is also felt among the clergy and religious. Nevertheless, we need to be creative in setting up possibilities for advance-

ment, at least recognizing some kinds of promotions after a specified number of years service. Clearly lay ministers with years of
dedicated service to a local church cannot be placed in the eyes of
the public as less important than the newest religious or cleric to
appear on the scene.

Ecclesial ministers must be encouraged to stay in their ministry,
and churches need to be prudent, visionary, and creative in finding
ways to show these dedicated Christian just how much we value
them.

Critical Issues When Ministering in Church Structures

Increasing Job Stability

The basic salary of most lay ecclesial ministers will be inadequate
to support a family, and its purchasing power may well decrease as
the years pass. Depending upon the kind of benefits that come with
the job, part of the salary may also have to be diverted to purchase
adequate insurance, pensions, and other professional benefits. Lay
ministers can supplement their salaries and may need to do so.
Career lay ministers, sensitive to the need to establish themselves
and foster stability in their ministry, can add other ministry outlets
to their basic ministerial responsibility. By doing so they can expand
their horizons, establish a fine reputation in the region, and also
increase their basic compensation. Many career lay ministers find
attendance at regional and national conferences excellent opportunities to establish a network that can provide new ideas for expanding
their outlets. The following are areas to pursue:

1. Form a speakers bureau throughout the diocese and surrounding region. Various lay ministers can offer to give evening presenta-
tions or workshops as guest speakers. Fees should be preestablished
and published along with the announcement of the services offered.

2. Introduce writing into your career. Parish-level publications
pay much more for articles than do scholarly journals. When you
initiate a new program, write up the process and an evaluation of it.
Others will certainly like to learn about it. If you need to give a
presentation to a group in your local church, write it up and send
it away for publication. Do not be concerned if your work is at first
rejected; try somewhere else.

3. Identify your own specialty, build up your experience, and make yourself available for consulting services in the region. Do not undervalue your competence and experience. Make sure your fees are set and known by those who contact you.

4. Document new projects you create and, besides writing about them, make the tools of the project available to others: handbooks, questionnaires, planning forms, evaluation reports, etc.

5. Set up a team of lay ministers to give parish retreats. Out of your experience you should be able to highlight needed areas of spiritual challenge and appropriate dynamics for parish renewal.

6. Knowing your own best skills, look into federal, state, or city programs that could utilize the same skills. Thus, a youth minister might contribute to a federal program for juveniles; a music minister might work in a nursing home; a staff member specializing in group dynamics or conflict management may find part-time work with the military or business community.

7. Add your own ideas and those of your friends and colleagues.

Some Useful Diocesan Experiences

Here are a series of reports and pastoral letters on the attempts of several dioceses to prepare and publish pastoral plans, to facilitate collegial government and a spirit of collaboration, to deal justly with employees, and to establish just forms of government for the resolutions of disputes in the Church. They present efforts made in the eighties, and some offer models that can be imitated or modified to suit differing regions.

Bishops of Minnesota. "Employers and Employees in the Church." *Origins* II (1981): 8–10.

Cosgrove, William, Bishop of Belleville, IL. "Resolving Disputes in the Church." *Origins* II (1981): 1–8.

Diocese of Oakland, CA. "Statement on Women in Ministry." *Origins* II (1981): 331–33.

Diocese of Raleigh, NC. "The Collegial Church." *Origins* 11 (1982): 721–24.

Diocese of Stockton, CA. "A Diocese Outlines Its Goals." *Origins* 11 (1981): 98–100.

Gerety, Peter, Archbishop of Newark, NJ. "Women in the Church." *Origins* 10 (1981): 582–88.

Head, Edward, Bishop of Buffalo, NY. "The Pilgrim Church of the '80s." *Origins* 11 (1982): 485–88.

Hemrick, Fr. Eugene, "Report on Church Personnel: Developments in Ministry." *Origins* 13 (1984): 561–66.

Hubbard, Howard, Bishop of Albany. "Planning in the Church: The People, the Tasks." *Origins* 12 (1983): 729–37.

Hughes, William, Bishop of Covington, KY. "How Responsibility is Shared: Not Lords, But Servants." *Origins* 15 (1986): 479–85.

———. "A Vision of the Church." *Origins* 12 (1982): 199–208.

Keating, John, Bishop of Arlington, VA. "Consultation in the Parish." *Origins* 14 (1984): 257–66.

Mahony, Roger, Archbishop of Los Angeles, CA. "A Church That Is Collaborative." *Origins* 16 (1987): 526–30.

Murphy, Thomas, Bishop of Great Falls-Billings, MT. "The Leadership Needed for Parish Renewal." *Origins* 12 (1983): 610–13.

———. "On Parish Councils and Lay Ministry." *Origins* 11 (1982): 648–51.

———. "Pastoral Planning: Issues of the '80s." *Origins* 12 (1982): 40–47.

Niedergeses, James, Bishop of Nashville, TN. "Governing a Local Church." Reprinted in *Origins* 9 (1980): 637–41.

"Recommendations of Chicago Laity Conference." *Origins* 11 (1981): 201–8.

Roach, John, Archbishop of St. Paul and Minneapolis, MN. "Practical Considerations: Sharing Responsibility." *Origins* 12 (1981): 15–16.

I recommend the following as excellent documents that individuals or dioceses may wish to use or imitate:

Anthony, Mark, Edith Austing, et al. "DREs: Who Do They Say We Are?" *Living Light* 23 (1986–87): 223–35. A research project on how parishioners view DREs, sponsored by the Religious Education Associations of Cincinnati and Dayton, OH.

Archdiocese of Milwaukee, Department of Christian Formation. Detailed job descriptions for over sixty diocesan-identified ministries have been developed. Each presents the position, summarizes the ministry, identifies responsibilities, and lists qualifications. These job descriptions are complemented with the archdiocesan mission statement and the Christian Formation Department's expectations of personnel in areas of commitment, collaboration, and communication.

Archdiocese of New York. "Process for Conciliation and Arbitration," New York, 1974.

Archdiocese of St. Paul and Minneapolis. *Personnel Guidelines for Church Ministry, 1987.* This is among the best diocesan publications, giving excellent examples of standards for professional competence, sample job descriptions, and sample forms for parish use in hiring, review, and termination. Distributed to every parish in the archdiocese in January 1987, these guidelines should be read by any diocese that has not yet published its own.

Charter of the Rights of Catholics in the Church, 3rd ed. Association for the Rights of Catholics in the Church Delran, N.J. 1987.

DeBoy, Jim, and Mary Margaret Funk. "Toward the Professionalization of DREs: Recommended Readings." *Living Light* 19 (1982): 250–53. A fine listing of resources for professionals: diocesan documents, books, and periodicals.

Diocese of Green Bay, WI. Their Mission Statement and Goals offers a clear presentation that is a helpful focus for any lay minister thinking of working in this diocese. Green Bay also has on file some fine parish mission statements and detailed job descriptions.

Diocese of Spokane, WA. Their Parish Personnel Handbook includes guidelines for hiring, check lists for job descriptions, sample lists of qualifications, steps in salary calculation, due process, mutual responsibilities.

Formation for Ministry. The Way Supplement 56 (1986). This issue includes a series of articles on various aspects of formation for ministry.

The National Association of Church Personnel Administrators (NACPA). *Just Treatment for Those Who Work for the Church.* Cincinnati, OH, 1986.

———. *Resources for Personnel Management.* Cincinnati, OH. This is a leaflet listing books and tapes.

Margaret O'Brien Steinfels, *Diverse Roles of the Laity in the Church's Mission and Community: A Report to the Raskob Foundation."* New York: National Pastoral Life Center, 1987.

Policy Changes in the Local Church to Protect Lay Ministers

Laity who have generally financed their own training, and work for low salaries, frequently find their security threatened. The Church cannot afford to lose these excellent ministers. The following are some suggestions of policy changes that could be made to assure laity of greater protection. Many dioceses have already established new policies that are models for others to learn from.

1. Compensation to lay ministers should be just. In fidelity to the Church's social teaching, and especially the recent challenge of the U.S. Bishop's Pastoral on the Economy, local churches can effectively reevaluate their compensation packages to lay ministers and

formally state the parish's commitment to justice. Let specialists within the parish community (middle managers, firm owners, personnel directors) evaluate parish practices and make recommendations. Where necessary, churches should undertake serious efforts to wean parishioners and parish council members away from the idea that ministry is gratuitous or at most is covered by a modest offering.

2. Let parishes, dioceses, and other ecclesial structures deal with lay ministers seriously and professionally. Contractual agreements, compensation packages, job responsibilities, annual evaluations, reasons for possible termination, and all other job-related interactions should be in writing and be reviewed by legal counsel (possibly a volunteer in the parish). Such legal advice may also be made available to the lay minister, especially if he or she is young, recently graduated, or inexperienced regarding the implications of professional agreements.

3. The local diocese does well to commit itself publicly to uphold justice by establishing due process and by stating the rights of a lay minister in regard to a new pastor who may not want a lay minister.

4. Slowly, and no doubt painfully, dioceses need to reeducate all personnel to the realization that a parish does not belong to a pastor to do as he wishes. He is one of several ministers, all of whom have rights.

5. Dioceses would do well to establish and publish common standards for salaries and benefits, lest a lay minister in a poor parish is treated differently than one in a wealthy parish. Common job descriptions would alleviate the burdens of ministers who are constantly expected to take on added responsibilities. Common directives can establish vacations, days off, and release time for extra commitments.

6. Since the parish belongs to the diocese and not the pastor, let visionary dioceses establish policy to deal with serious disagreements regarding the direction of the local church. Although at times bishops know the lay minister is the visionary and real spiritual leader in a parish, they allow a threatened pastor to oppose growth and accept the damage to the community.

Topics for Reflection and Discussion

Looking after Yourself as a Minister

Before You Accept a Position

	Yes	No	Comments
1. Did you feel welcome in the church when you visited?			
2. Does the local church (and its team) have a mission statement?			
3. Is there reasonable likelihood that this is, or can become, a collaborative team?			
4. In visiting staff members' offices were there signs that they kept professionally up to date? Journals? Books?			
5. Reflect on the relationships among team members: Was there a good give and take? Was a hierarchy clearly visible? Did the staff have regular meetings?			
6. In examining the church buildings, did the church itself portray liturgical renewal? Did the other rooms look well used? Were they conducive to what you would like to do?			
7. Was the office, pointed out to you as possibly yours, adequate and similar to the others?			
8. Would there be extreme differences between your understanding of Church and that of anyone on the staff?			

If you answered negatively to four of the above, give serious thought to refusing the position.

	Yes	No	Comments
1. Did the local church organization provide you with a job description?			
2. Are the lines of accountability clear?			

	Yes	No	Comments
3. Is there a contract?			
4. Is there provision for stability in case of a change of pastor?			
5. Are the maximum number of hours a week specified?			
6. Are days off indicated?			

If you answered no to any of 1–4, determine this information before proceeding.

	Yes	No	Comments
1. Is the salary adequate? Is there provision for cost of living increases? Is it clear how much you will be paid and at what intervals?			
2. Is pay comparable with other jobs in the neighborhood requiring the same skills? (Check at the town's employment bureau.)			
3. Is medical coverage included at a level similar to other diocesan workers?			
4. Is the contract for twelve months, ten months, or less?			
5. Check which of the following benefits are included: Pension plan Life insurance Worker's insurance Paid sick leave Annual paid vacation (two-three weeks)			
6. Are there professional benefits? Car Gas or mileage allowance Financial support for continuing education and workshops			

	Yes	No	Comments
Book budget			
Membership fees in professional organizations of lay ministers			
Travel allowance to educational or professional meetings			
Day-care facilities			
7. Was the office and its equipment adequate?			
8. Is there secretarial support staff?			

Lay ministers with financial obligations should prudently assure themselves of all the above. What is adequate is relative.

When Working as a Permanent Lay Minister	Yes	No	Comments
1. Do you have an updated job description?			
2. Do you have a current contract? How long is it for?			
3. Is your salary above the U.S. poverty level?			
4. Has salary kept pace with your professional development (e.g., degree completion) or personal responsibilities? (Maybe you have married since you began this position, or have children, house mortgage, etc.)			
5. What percentage increase in salary did you receive last year? Was it higher than the cost of living increase?			
6. When did you last receive a promotion?			
7. When were you most recently evaluated?			
8. Have you received any public recognition of your work?			
9. If other jobs were available besides this one, would you leave?			
10. Would your spouse prefer you had another job?			

	Yes	No	Comments
11. Are you happy, frustrated, angry?			
12. Has this position been an opportunity for spiritual growth?			
13. Do you experience any harassment from pastor or staff because of your theological views?			
14. Do you experience discrimination because you are lay or a woman?			
15. Are you consulted in matters concerning your area of responsibility?			
16. Do you find your staff members supportive?			

Questions for Group Sharing

1. Has lay ministry been as fulfilling as you hoped it would be?
2. Would you encourage others to dedicate themselves to lay ministry? What would you highlight as motives for their commitment?
3. Are you challenged, overchallenged, or underchallenged in your present ministry?
4. How does your ministry enhance the quality of your life or detract from it?
5. What are the principal tensions in your ministry?
6. What qualities do laity need for involvement in pastoral ministry?
7. What do you do to make a team experience productive and satisfying?
8. How long do you think you will stay in lay ministry, and what will you do when you leave?
9. What could be done to upgrade the image of the professional lay ecclesial minister in your local church?
10. Do people see you as a pastoral leader?

Some Concerns about Ministering in Church Structures Expressed by Lay Ministers

My ministry must change with every change of pastor. The areas of ministry stay almost the same but my style has to change.

•

We are asking for burnout of lay ministers! Work hours are not 9-5, although contracts are written to read as such. I end up working most evenings since that is when lay volunteers can come. Also supposedly paid holidays end up as working periods since that is when volunteers are free. What is going to happen to our family? Priests complain about missing their days off. When do they think families involved in lay ministry get their days off?

•

Structures without an articulated vision of building a kingdom of peace, love, and justice, have no future.

•

Our history has been that priests and religious were paid very little since they worked for love. But the Church also provided for their needs. Lay people in ministry need to be paid a living wage. Too often the only way lay people can minister is to be married to someone who earns the primary salary. Lay persons are on their own for expenses that priests and religious have as fringe benefits. Lay ministers usually have no provisions for retirement.

•

Structures squeeze the spontaneity out of my ministry.

•

We have no due process and the archbishop doesn't apologize for that in the least.

•

As a woman you have a sense of powerlessness in a male clerical world.

•

It is really a shame that persons who dedicate their lives and efforts to ministry in the Church community have to worry about salary or benefits. The injustice in Church communities is horrible and needs to be corrected. I don't think I am greedy. I would just like to pay off the thousands of dollars in student loan debts I have acquired trying to educate myself so I can serve the people of God.

Selected Reading

Barta, Russell, ed. *Challenge to the Laity.* Huntington, IN: Our Sunday Visitor, Inc., 1980.

Doohan, Leonard. *The Lay-Centered Church.* Harper & Row: San Francisco, 1984

Gremillion, Joseph, and Jim Castelli. *The Emerging Parish.* San Francisco: Harper & Row, 1987.

Hoge, Dean. *The Future of Catholic Leadership: Responses to the Priest Shortage.* Kansas City: Sheed and Ward, 1987.

Rauner, Judy. *Helping People Volunteer.* San Diego: Malborough Publishing Co., 1983.

Sweetser, Thomas, and Carol Wisniewski Holden. *Leadership in a Successful Parish.* San Francisco: Harper & Row, 1987.

Additional Reading

Doohan, Leonard. *The Laity: A Bibliography.* Wilmington, DE: Michael Glazier, Inc., 1987. See sections 16, 25, 26, 28, 36.

Chapter 5

LAY PASTORING

Lay Ministers Speak on Pastoring

Reflections

Introduction
The Changing Role of the Priestly Pastor
Career Lay Ministers as Pastoral Leaders
Qualities of Pastoral Leadership
Growth in Leadership
Pastoring and Presiding

Critical Issues for Lay Pastoral Ministers

Time Management
The Leader of the Future
Pastoral Skills

Topics for Reflection and Discussion

Reflection on Attitudes on Discussion and Dialogue
Questions for Personal Reflection
Questions for Group Sharing

Some Concerns about Pastoring Expressed by Lay Ministers

Selected Reading

Lay Ministers Speak on Pastoring

Pastoring—that's my work. Everyone brings their problems to me.

•

The Church will grow and change in healthy ways as more laity get involved. There is so much satisfaction in helping people. You have the chance to make a difference, to stand up against some of what society is teaching, doing, causing. Dedicating one's life to ministry brings closeness with God.

•

I see myself as an associate pastor, and so does the parish.

•

My pastoral ministry is definitely rewarding because over and over again I experience God's presence in the goodness and giftedness of others—the sharing enables us all to grow in holiness.

•

Pastoral advisors like me need good speaking ability, a sense of humor, ability to lead the prayer service, and interpersonal skills.

•

The fact that we can round up at least one hundred volunteers each year for catechetical ministry—I guess it says something!

Reflections

Introduction

We have reflected on the history of ministry, the contemporary emphasis on collaboration, and the resulting implications of shared ministry. Since this book deals with career lay ministers working internally to the Church, we considered some of the problems and opportunities that such commitment offers. The word "pastor," previously reserved for the ordained minister, is increasingly applicable to grass roots ministers. In fact, the Vatican Council's teaching on pastoral leadership is one of those areas that needs reinterpretation, as the concrete conditions of our local churches change. This chapter examines the changes in the priestly pastor's role and how this leads to the emergence of increased need for lay leadership in ministry. Career lay ministers are no longer just assistants. They must also give serious attention to those qualities of leadership that need to be part of their lives.

The Vatican Council's document on the Church stated: "For the nurturing and constant growth of the People of God, Christ the Lord instituted in His Church a variety of ministries, which work for the good of the whole body" (Church 18:1). To be ministers in the Church implies the gift and call of authority. Jesus seemingly was very clear in what he meant by authority, and this is reflected in the unanimous presentation of the New Testament writers. When two of the apostles demanded privileges of authority, Jesus replied: "You know that among the pagans the rulers lord it over them, and their great men make their authority felt. This is not to happen among you. No. Anyone who wants to be great among you must be your servant" (Matt. 20:25–28). There is only one occasion in scripture where authority means an unlimited right to act, and that is when Jesus claims that all authority in heaven and on earth is given to him (Matt. 28:18). Jesus returns to the original meaning of authority and bypasses the decadent worldly practices of it. "Anyone who wants to be first among you must be the servant of all" (Mark 9:35). Jesus reverses the relationship between serving and being served (Luke 22:27). Authority figures in Jesus' day were served, the ministers in his Church were definitely "set over" other members of the community, but they achieved their mission through service. Authority comes from the word "augere," which means to make someone grow. Ministers must have authority, i.e., must lead others to growth. St. Paul acted "with the authority which the Lord gave me for building up and not for destroying" (2 Cor. 13:10). To the Corinthians, he said: "Maybe I do boast rather too much about my authority, but the Lord gave it to me for building you up and not for pulling you down, and I shall not be ashamed of it" (2 Cor. 10:8). Understood in the New Testament way, it is a delight that there are key ministers who were called to lead the rest of us to growth, and no pastor should in these democratic days be ashamed of it. The functions of the key ministers of the Church are documentable in scripture and generally synthesized in the call to govern, teach, preach and sanctify. These functions imply a call to authority, in other words, a call to further the growth of others. The question is how can this be realistically done today.

One important task that is always before the Church is to make present the living Word of God to every generation. This implies a double function—self-criticism and interpretation. The self-critical task means that the Church must measure everything by scripture. However, that is not enough. We must also carry out the interpretational task which means to reincarnate the message, to interpret Jesus' message for our own age. We can't afford to be conservatives who do not reinterpret the message, nor progressives who break away from that past which is Jesus'. However, Jesus' life and message were spirit and life for the people of his time, and we make them spirit and life for people today. We change in order to be the same. If we remain as we were in a previous generation, we will not be to our present one the life-giving challenge our predecessors were to their own.

If the pastor is to be to us today and tomorrow what the priestly pastor was to our predecessors, then the role of pastor changes, and pastoral functions modify, thus insuring that the ministry will be the same.

Responding to the need for a changed model of the pastor, like any paradigm shift, is fraught with difficulties: differences of opinion, polarization, fear, frustration, and insecurity. However, if we believe in the central significance of the pastor to each generation, then the need for a new model of pastoral ministry becomes the Lord's call echoing for those who have heard it before.

The Changing Role of the Priestly Pastor

My wife and I give workshops together, and recently we gave one on lay ministry in a Canadian diocese. On Saturday morning, the pastor received the sad news that his father had died in Ireland, and after the urging of a fellow priest from a nearby parish, he decided to return for the funeral. Before leaving he pointed out two lay eucharistic ministers in the audience. Attending the workshop was the priest of the next parish, who pointed out to the people that he had several Masses the next day, all in different locations, and would be unable to celebrate the Eucharist for them. He then added: "Yesterday was the twenty-first anniversary of my ordination, and I would like you to realize I am the most recently ordained priest in the diocese." The next day, Pentecost Sunday, the laity managed the services on their own. For many contemporary Christians, Sunday worship is a priestless function, and this is not only true of small rural parishes, but equally an experience in a growing number of city parishes.

When I hear people quoting negative statistics about marriage, I feel discouraged, and I'm sure priests do when they hear negative statistics regarding the priesthood repeated over and over again. However, as Church, we not only need to face up to these negative trends, we also need to savor the pain and learn to grieve, for it is out of such pain that true valuing of the priesthood can grow.

The decrease in priestly ministers is severe in the United States. The United States now has half the number of priests it had at the turn of the century, but four times the number of Catholics. Today we have one priest for every 1,500 Catholics, but by the year 2000 each priest will have to minister to a minimum of 4,000 people—I say a minimum because the official statistics include priests of all ages, including retired. Even before the end of this decade most priests will have to take on the added responsibilities of another parish besides their current ministerial obligations. Some dioceses set ministry goals and find that the decreases in clergy that they expected within ten years have already occurred.

Resignations, which continue in spite of Vatican refusal to grant dispensations, intensify this bleak picture. Twenty percent of the priests who were active in 1968 have now left the priestly ministry. The United States will soon have as many resigned priests as active ones, and if trends continue, there will always be more resigned priests than active ones. Priests in every diocese are aware of the changing median age, which has increased throughout the nation to about fifty and is rising each year.

While there are always outstanding exceptions, we also acknowledge that the quality of many incoming seminarians is not what it used to be: their studies, psychological maturity, and interpersonal skills leave much to be desired. The ultraconservatism of many is a national concern. Sadly we acknowledge that statistics already show that priesthood is a vocation that many people with the necessary qualities are no longer choosing.

Up to the seventies the priest held a position of great respect. A man of stature in the city or community, he was considered one of the educated people of the area, an expert, a talented spiritual leader, a man of authority with a very healthy self-image. Nowadays it is possible to find priestly pastors less theologically educated than some of their parishioners; priestly pastors who were trained for one kind of leadership, but must live another; priestly pastors who answered a call to use their priestly talents, but actually spend over 80 percent of their time in managerial tasks for which they had no particular calling and may not have the skills. They find themselves at times called to uphold theologically and morally what they personally don't accept. Their authority is questioned, their influence diminishing, their self-concept not what it was.

In the past, the celibate life was considered spiritually more perfect, ascetically more demanding, and ministerially more effective. Dedicated married laity have shown beyond question that ministerial availability and dedication are not related to celibacy. Moreover, the challenges to build a lasting Christian marriage are at times ascetically more demanding than celibacy, and although recent Church documents insist that celibacy is "a state of perfection," most laity have the nagging feeling that this is a political statement to help maintain current structures more than a spiritual reality. Speaking to a group of priests last year, I tried to stress the evangelical value of celibacy for the kingdom. One of them, claiming to voice the opinion of the majority, said I would have great difficulty in finding one priest in the diocese in question who would affirm that celibacy was a positive contribution to his spiritual life. No one challenged his intervention.

Historically the clergy were a privileged class, rewarded with larger parishes, honorary titles, and financial control. Now many priestly pastors reject larger parishes to work with smaller groups. Many of the smaller pool of clerical pastors become circuit riders, and others, even though close to retirement, are uprooted to serve elsewhere. In one of his earlier works, Fr. William Bausch spoke about the pastor governing an American parish that he saw as composed of eight layers of a pyramid—the lowest bottom layer being ethnic immigrant. Now increasing numbers of parishes are served by pastors who are recent ethnic immigrants.

Even as recent as a generation ago, the vast majority of an individual's religious needs were satisfied in the parish by the pastor. Nowadays people have new needs that they see as integral to their religious growth and turn outside of the parish for the skills and services of other laity or religious women.

Studies on trends in the nation and the Church, such as John Naisbitt's *Megatrends* or Richard Schoenherr's statistical studies of the Catholic Church, or Catholic University sociologist Dean Hoge's research, emphasize the decreased importance of hierarchies, the rejection of male exclusivity, and the refusal to participate in structures that do not share power. These studies also stress the verified trends of networking, intervocational ministry, new styles of local leadership, and the increased importance of collaboration. Moreover, since the local reality is more important to people than the international administration, they all imply that leadership is viewed differently than in the past and may well be identified in Christians other than the priest, leaving the latter in an exclusively managerial role.

The central role of the priest as sacramental minister is also changing in people's minds, due partly to the decreased availability of the Eucharist and to the increased importance of the proclamation of the Word. It is difficult to maintain the centrality of the Eucharist when laity see that celibacy is actually considered to be more important.

Priests consist of .5 percent of the Catholic population. In the past they were unquestionably the best trained and the most dedicated. Nowadays there are certainly more than 2 percent of the Catholic laity who are knowledgeable, well trained, and very dedicated—2 percent is more than all priests and religious men and women combined. The picture of declining numbers, status, and future prospects is discouraging regarding traditional priestly ministry.

Career Lay Ministers as Pastoral Leaders

Since the sixties, the shortage of ministers increasingly has been filled with professionally trained laity. Many of these postconciliar pioneers faced initial rejection, but directors of religious education and youth ministers made such a positive impact on parish life that they became permanent features of the local structures and blazed the trail for further specialization in ministries.

"Lay ministry" is a term that needs further specification and "professional lay ministry" fails to respect the vocational component of the life. Some officials wish to establish more clearly defined perimeters of lay involvement and channels of control. Others, like many participants in the Synod on the Laity prefer not to talk about career lay ministers, perhaps hoping that they will just go away. Fortunately for the needy and priestless faithful, a remarkable number of laity dedicate themselves to pastoral ministry. Fortunately for the institutional Church, they show more interest and faithful respect for the Church than they receive. Nevertheless, career lay ministers can expect to play increasingly important roles in the Church.

A recent exploratory survey found that lay men and women ministering in parishes, diocesan offices, and a wide range of Christian agencies identified "political issues," such as clericalism, sexism, problems with authorities and structures as the most critical, emotionally intense issues they have to deal with. Concern about their own careers in relation to institutional Church followed, then work-related emotional issues and employment issues (Marian Schwab, "Career Lay Ministers," *Today's Parish,* October 1987, 9–10).

There is no leadership until there are followers who believe in what the leader believes in. Career lay ministers have gradually received respectful acceptance and now lead some of the most successful parishes, or parish programs, in the nation. In fact, some priestless communities are among the best, offering wonderful experiences of Church. To the question "Are lay pastors a parishable breed?" (Brian Baker, *U.S. Catholic* 46 [August 1981]: 31–37), the votes are in, and the answer is—they definitely are!

Career lay ministers as pastoral leaders help ease current pressures of decreased clergy and sometimes bring a different perspective to parish life, but this does not necessarily change the parish problems. Lay leaders face the same problems that clergy do. Before pastoring successfully, lay leaders need a clear understanding of the nature of the Church and the purpose of the parish, an awareness of local needs, and a vision of the role of all laity. If they work in a team, they can never presume that roles are clear. It is important to talk through each one's understanding of roles.

Lay leaders will have the same struggles with models of pastoral leadership as clerical pastors have had: are they coordinators, providers of services, focal points for a shared vision, managers, spiritual directors, or something else? Laity dedicating themselves to pastoring and pastoral ministry are entering a ministry that was not redefined by Vatican II. The Council said a lot about bishops, laity, and religious, but not about pastoring, even in its two documents on the priesthood. Thus, pastoral models develop reactively without a unified vision. While I do not think that a clear understanding of the nature of the priesthood is attainable until after much more has been done on the life and mission of laity, nevertheless a clearer focus on pastoring is possible. Thus, a recent National Catholic Conference of Bishops' study on the role of pastor helps all in pastoral ministry, even though it presumes it is speaking about priests (*A Shepherd's Care: Reflections on the Changing Role of Pastor* [Washington, DC: National Catholic Conference of Bishops, 1987]). The involvement of career lay ministers will not only redefine the meaning of pastor, but will aid in a renewed understanding of the priesthood.

Lay pastoral ministers are exploring new models of pastoring that the Church may eventually institutionalize. As they recognize their strengths, compensate for their weaknesses, and nurture their skills, the question is no longer if we will have lay pastors but how will they pastor? These laity, a genuine resource for ministry, are marshaling skills through networking, pilot projects, and tentative solutions. Their experimentation in pastoral leadership on a one to one basis, or with small cell groups fosters ownership of parish by the people and transforms their own roles too.

Like all leaders, these new pastoral ministers need vision and skills. They must implement four key strategies: the management of peoples' attention through focusing on a compelling vision; the management of shared understanding of faith through communication; the management of trust through their own integrity, stability, and reliability; and the management of themselves through self-respect, confidence, and faithful dedication (Warren Bennis and Burt Nanus, *Leaders* [New York: Harper & Row, 1985]).

Lay leaders have learned from successful priestly pastors how to care, trust, and support their people; how to identify, release, and unify the gifts of all; how to plan, organize, and motivate the community. The generosity of our priests is now a quality so easily identified with career lay ministers who share the priest's hunger for the peoples' growth and are always ready to go the extra mile to spark interest in others, inspire them, or channel their dedicated vision.

The Holy Spirit who calls ministries into life in the Church is blessing our generation with a variety of dedicated career lay ministers who are responding to the needy faithful. These pastoral leaders are well trained and clearly experienced in their ministry.

Qualities of Pastoral Leadership

Leadership is a process not a person and the individual leader is the one who has the ability to make things happen. He or she has a strong commitment to the group and, in fact, works harder for the group's effectiveness than the followers do. A good leader influences others, taps their charisms, unites them, and awakens them to their own call. A great leader makes conscious what lies unconscious in the followers. In time a great leader can withdraw, having trained others to lead themselves. As the Chinese mystic Lao-tzu says: "Of the best leaders, when their task is accomplished, the people all remark, 'We have done it ourselves.' "

The contemporary pastoral leader requires a high degree of self-esteem, creativity, and integrity, together with an ability to accept conflict, a willingness to be unloved, and prudence to pick the issues worthy of confrontation. He or she eliminates the pathological aspects of institutions (fear, hostility, dependency, loss of motivation), breaks away from bureaucratic ideas, accepts all into leadership positions, commits himself or herself to participation, and possesses enthusiasm for life. He or she communicates well, controls his or her own prejudices, keeps all well informed, praises freely, cares for people, helps coworkers, builds independence, exhibits a willingness to learn, shows confidence in others, facilitates freedom of expression, and delegates, delegates, delegates.

The leadership style of a pastor speaks less of managerial ability and more of faith, particularly ecclesiology. From the way a pastor runs a parish, it is relatively easy to determine his or her understanding of the nature of the Church and the quality of his or her faith.

Leaders today in all walks of life are in search of excellence. Christian pastoral leaders must be so too. If they are not gifted with the vision or the skills of leadership, they can commit themselves to self-development in leadership styles that are appropriate ways of demonstrating shared responsibility in the eighties and nineties.

Above all, the pastoral leader is a person of faith—a faith that constantly seeks deeper understanding. This implies ongoing study of one's faith, or return to study for those who have abandoned it. It requires prolonged contact with God in prayer and deep sharing with others. Study, prayer, and sharing will keep faith from becoming pseudofaith that is nothing more than the embodiment of our own psychological needs. Dedication to faith cannot be presumed but rather becomes the basis of daily recommitment.

The Vatican Council appealed for people who could give us reasons for living and reasons for hoping. In times of crisis, polarization, and frustration, the pastoral leader is a person of hope, able to implement Christ's vision in a new way and to inspire others. His or her own spirituality needs to react against the oppression experienced by their peers but also manifest the joy and enthusiasm that comes from carrying burdens for Christ.

The leader's authority, based in personality rather than office, gives rise to a community of Christian love. The leader is the living principle of unity and facilitates community in others. After all, a pastoral leader is not dedicated to a structure or a theology but to people.

Deep faith, hope, and love complement and permeate the leadership qualities we have seen. Christian' struggle to find a convincing model of Christian leader is a paschal experience, a part of our contemporary living of the cross of the Lord. Gregory of Nyssa said that Christianity was a movement from beginnings to beginnings through beginnings that never ends. We see the truth of that insight in leaders today who face new roles, try to deal with new trends, and embody their perennial ministry in new forms. However, these years of change are particularly severe. In the book of Revelation, Jesus tells one of the local churches, "I have opened in front of you a door that nobody will be able to close" (Rev. 3:8). I believe an open door lies in front of us today. I doubt it will ever close again in a return to the way things used to be, but we need a lot of courage to walk through that door and become the pastoral leaders that tomorrow's Church needs.

Growth in Leadership

In *Redemptor Hominis,* John Paul II applies Vatican II's restricted understanding of collegial government more broadly than ever before, to priests in their councils and laity in their organizations. The leadership and governmental model offered to the Church is collegial.

Living collegially is a profound spiritual challenge. For the person in authority, governing in this way is a process of personal rebirth. Through such people the Church gives an increasingly clearer revelation of its mission. Collegial government requires in all authority figures a deep sense of belonging to the Church and an appreciation of those who make up the local church. It also requires in each leader an awareness of poverty, need of mutual help, and a spirit of trust with other Christians.

When we look at a collegial style of leadership, the authority figures are in process of becoming who they are called to be. It takes a matter of weeks to nominate a person to a position of authority, but it will be years before he or she becomes the leader of a particular group, the pastor of a local church—knowing it, loving it, serving it, feeling for it, suffering for it, knowing its people, working for their hopes, forming a community, giving a vision. Call is easy; the fulfillment of it is a life's mission, and we must sadly acknowledge that some never attain it.

We are all accustomed to stages of growth in life, whether personal or communal. We are also accustomed to stages of growth in spiritual life, prayer, and ongoing conversion. There are also stages of growth in leadership.

Is it Christian leadership to be an autocrat, a benevolent dictator, a paternalistic or maternalistic figure, or a leader who lets everyone do what they like? I think not. What then makes leadership *Christian* leadership? It's not a position in the Church, since many are positions of management and not leadership. It's not hierarchical office, since we all know of popes, bishops, priests, deacons, religious, or laity who were dictators. It's not belonging to a religious community and not even baptism—since some of the most oppressive regimes in the world are run by Christians.

We need a singleminded dedication to grow at all costs, convinced that our leadership style portrays our faith. Robert Greenleaf, addressing Christian leadership today, says that in some cases survival is now considered a brilliant performance. That minimalistic view is insufficient. Rather, like many professionals today, we must be in search of excellence in our Christian leadership style.

Leaders can be categorized as autocrats, benevolent autocrats, bureaucrats, and laissez-faire—none of which are Christian. Each stage contains vision and skills. There comes a time in leadership ministry when a crisis situation calls forth new leadership. First comes the vision of participatory forms of government, and later, sometimes but unfortunately not always, there follows the acquisition of new skills. Those pastoral leaders who fail to acquire new skills generally abandon their new vision and return to autocratic leadership styles. (See Brian P. Hall and Helen Thompson, *Leadership Through Values* [New York: Paulist Press, 1980]).

Those who are attracted by a new vision of participatory leadership are people who have a good balance of task-oriented skills and interpersonal skills; they are men and women who have integrated knowledge, intimacy, peer support, and team support in their ministerial commitment; they are men and women endowed with creative skills and caring skills. These new creative and caring skills are specifically Christian and allow a person to become a servant leader; they are participatory or collegial in style.

It is important that we all become more aware of our Christian calling to leadership development. We can reflect on our own leadership and acknowledge that one can be converted on many levels while still living a pagan or primitive form of leadership. Nowadays, Christian leaders proclaim to the world a Christian style of servant leadership at a time when this world's so-called leaders are lording it over their subjects, as Jesus anticipated they would. Now more than ever, one's level of leadership is a great indication of one's faith.

Collegial authority, an expression of faith, is a specifically Christian form of authority and leadership; it is an ecclesial response to Jesus' call for servant leadership by those baptized in his name. Blessed with equal dignity in baptism, and called to live a shared responsibility for faith, Christians throughout history have embodied that commitment to shared responsibility in a hierarchically structured Church. The shared responsibility of all the faithful expresses itself in those chosen from among the people of God to be leaders for them. Hierarchy is not a constitutive component of pastoral leadership, but shared responsibility is. Shared responsibility is a constitutive component of Christian leadership style. It is not possible to think of Christian leadership outside of shared responsibility. This requires service, dialogue, courtesy, and discernment. The leader cannot be self-reliant but searches for the consensus of all the community, and when he or she finds it, knows it is the decision of his or her greater self. In the Church, the individual leader is not important—after all, he or she can be replaced in a matter of weeks—rather what is important is who the leader becomes for the local church through interaction with followers.

We are told by the Council that "all share a true equality with regard to the dignity and to the activity common to all the faithful for the building up of the Body of Christ" (Church 32: 3). God's gifts are for all, and "in their diversity all bear witness to the admirable unity of the Body of Christ" (Church 32:4). This unity lived in the early Church is fostered in our communities, and "the individual bishop . . . is the visible principle and foundation of unity in his particular church" (Church 23:1). He is aided in his work by pastors, religious, and laity. All contribute, and "through the common effort to attain fullness in unity, the whole and each of the parts receive increase" (Church 13:3).

Leadership belongs to the group, and it is the group's responsibility to see that appropriate leadership is exercised. This Christian leadership of shared responsibility manifests itself in new ways today, demanding new leadership qualities from contemporary pastoral leaders.

Pastoring and Presiding

Many churches have now separated pastoring and presiding. Priests preside; in fact, some priests who must selflessly give themselves as sacramental circuit riders often only preside, and much pastoring is left to laity or religious women. The lay pastoral leader helps to redirect a previous overconcern with the presider to a new concern with the community. This refocusing is healthy since good quality community life can stimulate good pastoring.

The responsibilities of lay pastoral leaders are many. In collaboration with the people, they create a new and compelling vision, develop commitment to the vision, and institutionalize the vision. Lay pastoral leaders are resource people for the vision, teachers who can facilitate commitment, and organizers who can institutionalize the shared hopes of the community. They plan everything carefully and yet are skilled enough not to need prepackaged programs, confident to participate in some groups without a preconceived plan. Always learners, they are open to receive what they do not know at all.

Lay pastoral ministers are increasingly responsible for the unity and catholicity of the Church. As they accept increasing responsibilities, it is crucial that they foster a spirit of unity with the priest who may be absent, traveling to other parishes, a little out of touch, or approaching retirement. It is particularly difficult to maintain unity with the priestly hierarchy when the local priest is disgruntled with change and unaccepting of the "new breed." Issues that could degenerate into fear and anger may not lead the lay pastoral leader away from the obligation to build unity and maintain a sense of identity with the diocesan and universal Church. This prophetical ministry is a learning experience with significant value on an ecumenical level too as the lay leader deepens the skills of working for unity.

The practice of reserving presiding to the priestly minister can no longer be retained in many dioceses outside major urban areas, as increasing numbers of career lay ministers preside as part of their pastoral responsibilities. They preside over social functions, administrative and planning meetings such as the parish council, gatherings for spiritual development such as evenings of prayer or parish retreats, and community liturgical celebrations such as Bible and communion services.

The presiding pastoral leader develops new skills for presiding. These include clarity in speech, ability to articulate a message in an understandable way for many people at different levels of education, an excellent grasp of the sources of faith, a pleasant and welcoming attitude, a total rejection of all sexist language and attitudes, a sense of presence to the community, and a humble awareness that it is the community that is the real celebrant.

The presider reveals the Word to the people, interprets it, proclaims its present relevance, and acts as a catalyst challenging the community to ongoing conversion. The presider is the last link in the chain of interpretation stretching from Jesus' message to present-day listeners, and the presider can renew the covenant or the presider can thwart the proclamation in this final moment. Aware that he or she can be prophet or false prophet intensifies a sense of humility and a realization of the need to be knowledgeable in the faith.

The leader presiding over the community is a person of peaceful and loving acceptance of each member of the community. At the same time, the presider lives in a state of sustained hope for the community, always yearning and striving to make it better. The presider is teacher, connector, recognizer of gifts, organizer, challenger, allower, wisdom person, joymaker, discerner, enabler, or mourner (Dennis Geaney, *Emerging Lay Ministries* [Kansas City: Andrews & McMeel, Inc., 1979], 17–19).

The lay presider is a person of stature in the community. Maintaining an open and affirming style, always caring for persons under stress, the presider is a theologian in life and thought who leads the congregation in the development of their community spirit and faith. The ministry of presider grows from one's personal commitment in faith and calls both oneself and others to the service of the community and the world. The presider becomes more collegial in style and organization and ever more sensitive to the denominational characteristics of the community (David S. Schuller, ed., *Ministry in America* [San Francisco: Harper & Row, 1980], 23–53).

Like St. Paul, lay pastoral leaders carry the burdens of the churches. Sensitive to developments in the churches around the world, they are pained by divisions and polarizations. As they read journals and religious newspapers, they live and relive the nasty opposition that Christians show to other Christians. It is heartrending to preside over a divided local church and an equally bitter experience to see the division in the international Church. In increasing numbers, laity are drawn into struggles of the world Church, and, with little likelihood of major changes in the foreseeable future, they follow Christ's lead in praying to the Father: "It is for these that I sanctify myself" (John 17:19).

Critical Issues for Lay Pastoral Ministers

Time Management

Pastoral ministry requires extraordinary amounts of time and energy. The minister can become exhausted satisfying people's urgent needs. Before anyone should attempt to lead or manage other people's lives, one should be skilled in leading and managing one's own. Some unskilled but generous visionaries center their lives on their ministry and within a year have an unbalanced lifestyle that borders on exhaustion. Twenty-four-hour availability is not the way to maintain peak performance nor to assure long term effective ministerial dedication. The following seven components of time management can help maintain self-renewal and balance.

1. Guide your own life. Career lay ministers should not allow situations to control their lives, no matter how demanding they may be. The first application of management skills is to own one's life.
2. Establish priorities. In time of reflection or retreat, establish life-direction, personal, family, career, and job priorities. Each set of priorities is different.
3. Set long-term goals. For each of the priorities, list goals for the next five years.
4. Focus on this year's objectives. Given your hopes for the next five years, identify specific objectives for the upcoming year.
5. Plan a daily schedule. Set up an appropriate daily schedule based on the conclusions to the previous four questions. Decide how many hours of each day should be given to the specifics of your present job, your career goals, family or personal life, general direction of your life.
6. Manage the day. Within the time you allocate to your work, prioritize tasks, decide what deserves time, and what does not, deal with the important issues first, do not let the demands of others, including team members, consistently misdirect or consume the day.
7. Evaluation. Regularly rethink the above, readjust if necessary, identify weaknesses, and plan again.

Management of time is hindered by a series of time wasters that are frequently found among ministers. The following are time wasters for ministers. A lack of planning and prioritizing, together with an inability to say no to those ever-surfacing problems, consumes the minister's time. This often leads to management by crisis, in which each new problem gets immediate attention. The sense of vocation leads some to attempt too much, wanting to meet every need as soon as it arises. This is seen particularly in hasty responses to urgent requests, responses that are unplanned and time-consuming. Some waste time in open-ended meetings, an exaggerated concern for paperwork, nonselective reading, unnecessary socializing, and trivia. The desire to be dedicated to new forms of collaborative ministry gives rise in some to too much sharing and discussion, staff or leadership indecision, and a lack of delegation.

The Leader of the Future

As career lay ministers see themselves called to a greater involvement in situations that call for leadership qualities, it is important to realize that leadership includes both vision and skills, and the latter can be identified and areas of needed growth corrected by serious self-direction. A leader possesses enthusiasm for life and can enthuse others with the same interests. Such a leader reaffirms human values with an expressed faith in growth, change, and maturity, and establishes new directions for the future. He or she is committed to reasonable participation instead of power plays, is concerned with the elimination of pathological aspects within an institution (e.g., fear, hostility, dependency, loss of motivation), sees tension, conflict, dialogue, disagreement, and controversy as part of life, and acts even though unpopular decisions may need to be made. The leader for tomorrow's Church revitalizes motivation by tapping resources, uniting participants, and exhibiting confidence in collaborators. Thus, the leader presents an expansive view of work and orchestrates a network of responses, breaks away from bureaucratic roles (e.g., writing reports, attending meetings), and accepts all into leadership positions (women and minorities). This kind of leader is identified as a talented, articulate spokesperson, with the skill and vision to be a transforming leader, who demonstrates a creative, life-oriented leadership. (See Edna Mitchell, "Educational Leadership: Confronting Crises with Style" in Kathryn Cirincione-Coles, ed. *The Future of Education* [Beverly Hills, CA. Sage Publications, 1981], 35–42.)

Pastoral Skills

In addition to general skills of leadership, group dynamics, and knowledge of the faith, ministers need to acquire other skills to enrich their pastoral effectiveness, particularly the relational skills of quality presence to others. A minister needs to dress appropriately, neatly, and professionally, demonstrate self-control, and attention to others. This quality presence manifests respect for others by welcoming them, looking at them, and taking leave of them. A leader develops listening skills that show attentiveness, demonstrates hospitality through an ability to welcome all and make everyone feel at home, fosters a sense of community and draws people into the group. Such a person can use gestures to manifest appropriate attitudes—a smile, handshake, or eye contact. These relational skills help the leader create appropriate moods of joy, concern, sorrow, respect, or enthusiasm.

A leader's pastoral skills include not only relational, or unitive skills, but also communication skills. A leader must be able to speak clearly to individuals, small groups, and large groups and be able to articulate ideas for people at varied levels of education. The leader needs to be able to project voice and presence in a large meeting and to be comfortable in establishing eye contact with the audience, no matter its size. A pastoral leader is at ease with the poor, sick, handicapped, and people in authority; can make public announcements briefly, clearly, and pleasantly; and always retains a sense of the appropriate use of time, adequate, unhurried, and not exaggerated.

Spiritual leadership skills are also necessary for today's grass roots pastors. They must be at ease proclaiming scripture clearly and challengingly; praying publicly for the group, spontaneously or according to ritual; inviting others to pray; and talking about spiritual matters without embarassment. These spiritual leadership skills will include the liturgical skills of performing liturgical gestures gracefully: outstretched hands, imposition of hands, bows, offering communion, use of hands, touching objects and people, and creating an atmosphere of silence, reflection, praise, wonder, reverence.

Topics for Reflection and Discussion

Reflection on Attitudes on Discussion and Dialogue

In a Discussion

- Speak openly; it is your discussion.
- Listen attentively.
- Avoid monopolizing the discussion; speak when necessary.
- Avoid interrupting another.
- Avoid remaining outside the discussion or giving others the impression that you are not interested in what they have to say.
- If you disagree with something, say so.
- Come prepared as a service to the group.
- Reflect on who does the talking.
- Do you just discuss with your peer group?

– If you are dissatisfied with your group, say so to the group and give reasons.
– What does the group think of you?
– At the end of a group session, think over the period and see who spoke and why.
– What have you learned from those in the group who are less knowledgeable in certain areas than yourself?
– What consideration have you given in the way you speak to those who are more experienced?
– Avoid too many anecdotes and examples.
– Stir a response in love and good works.
– Rotate the service of group leader.
– Rotate the service of group secretary.

In Dialogue

– Do I presume the good will of others?
– Is there an attitude of trust within myself, or am I constantly questioning others' sincerity?
– Is my attitude one of defending or sharing?
– Do I believe each person has something to share?
– Am I putting people in boxes, categorizing?
– Do I feel there are many ways of experiencing and expressing truth?
– Am I holding onto my idea, or do I admit the possibility that I too can change and grow?
– Am I willing to initiate, to begin again even on painful topics?
– Am I willing to share my person and not just ideas?
– In listening, am I sensitive to what is said, unsaid? Do I listen to the heart, to the whole person?
– Am I committed to the persons I share with? Am I willing to help them grow?
– Do I invite persons to share, or do I threaten them because of my arrogance or defensiveness?
– Do I resist confrontation because of fear, wanting to be popular, or lack of love?
– Do I cut people off by words or attitudes?
– Am I too selective in what I share and with whom I share?
– Am I growing in openness to others?

Questions for Personal Reflection

On Shared Ministry

1. Who is a person I admire or identify with in contemporary Church ministry?

2. In what ways has my service of others in ministry expressed my truest self?

3. What needs in our Church and/or society call for a personal response from me?

4. What gifts for ministry has God given me?

5. What obstacles prevent me from developing and using these gifts?

6. What most helps me to be effective in my ministry?

7. Do I create space for the prophets in the group?

On Christian Leadership

1. What do you expect of leaders in the Church?
2. What do you expect of followers within the Church?
3. Where would you place yourself, among leaders or followers?
4. How do you anticipate your leadership and ministry changing in the next five years?
5. What is leadership within the context of Church?
6. How would you distinguish between a leader and leadership?
7. What makes the exercise of leadership Christian?
8. Why do you think people need you?
9. Why do you think Christ needs you in this ministry?
10. Why do you need to do this ministry?

Questions for Group Sharing

1. How do you think the Church can cope with the decrease in the numbers of clergy? How do you think the Church will deal with it?
2. What is essential in the role of pastor? Name the five main services you hope the pastoral minister will satisfy for you. Do the five services require ordination?
3. How can laity help the priest and be affirming of priestly ministry?
4. Would you like one of your children to be a priest? If so, why? If not, why not? Would you like one of your children to be involved in pastoral ministry? If so, why? If not, why not?

5. What do you contribute to your parish? What do you expect from your parish?
6. Describe an ideal parish: its style of life, goals, services, and ministers.
7. Did Jesus ordain priests? Have laity ever celebrated the Eucharist? Have religious ever ordained others?
8. Describe the forms of ecclesiastical structure found in the New Testament.
9. To what extent have changes in your parish improved or weakened it?
10. Who are the pastors who have had the most positive influence on your life? What did you like about them?

Some Concerns about Pastoring Expressed by Lay Ministers

Some lay ministers are very dedicated to their work, others are not. Some are committed to their own work with no interest in anyone else's ministry and see no ecclesiological problem with this.

•

I perform all the functions of a pastor except the sacraments, but others don't see me as a pastor—we're moving slowly.

•

I have had horrendous freedom in my ministry. However, I constantly deal with being a second-class citizen in certain matters to do with spirituality by parishioners who are very hierarchical in their ways of thinking.

•

If pastor is defined as one who serves the Church, then I see myself as a pastor. If pastor is defined as priest or clergyman, then no.

Selected Reading

Bannon, William J., and Suzanna Donovan. *Volunteers and Ministry.* New York: Paulist Press, 1983.

Chandler, Mary Moisson. *The Pastoral Associate and the Lay Pastor.* Collegeville, MN: The Liturgical Press, 1986.

Diocese of Nelson, British Columbia. *Guidelines for Lay Presiders,* 1987.

Doohan, Helen. *Leadership in Paul.* Wilmington, DE: Michael Glazier, Inc., 1984.

Gilmour, Peter. *The Emerging Pastor: Non-Ordained Catholic Pastors.* Kansas City, MO: Sheed & Ward, 1986.

Henderson, Frank J. "Liturgical Skills." *National Bulletin on Liturgy* 17 (May/June 1984): 178–82.

Rockers, Dolore, and Kenneth J. Pierre. *Shared Ministry: An Integrated Approach to Leadership and Service.* Winona, MN: St. Mary's Press, 1984.

Western Liturgical Conference of Canada. *Ritual for Lay Presiders,* rev. ed. Ottawa: Canadian Catholic Conference of Bishops, 1981.

Additional Reading

Doohan, Leonard. *The Laity: A Bibliography.* Wilmington, DE: Michael Glazier, Inc., 1987. See sections 24, 29, 37, 39.

Chapter 6

MEETING TENSIONS IN MINISTRY

L̶ay Ministers Speak About Tensions in Ministry

Reflections

Introduction
Renewal through Ministry
Initial Problems and Tensions in Ministry
Tensions Resulting from the Different Understandings of Ministry Held by the Minister and the Community
Forces against Effective Leadership in Ministry
Surviving Tensions in Ministry
A Concluding Reflection on Tensions in Ministry

Critical Issues and Tensions in Ministry

Conflict management
Burnout in Ministry
A Self-Test for Satisfaction in One's Work

Topics for Reflection and Discussion

A Personal Review of One's Ministry: Questions for Personal Meditation
Questions for Group Sharing

Some Concerns of Lay Ministers about Tensions in Ministry

Selected Reading

Lay Ministers Speak on Tensions in Ministry

When you work someplace where you're unhappy, you tend to carry unhappiness with you everywhere. But the opposite is true also. If you're happy and you know it, let it show. I think mine does.

•

I receive support from my family, from other women working in the Church, and also from women friends not working in the Church.

•

The principal stress in my ministry is too much work.

•

My supports are my pastor, my remarkably patient and funny family (husband and two teenage daughters), my circle of great friends, my coworkers, and many diocesan priests.

•

I really didn't know what ministry would be like, and I really didn't think of reward, but I do get a lot of satisfaction from my interaction with others in ministry.

•

We need patience, strong support from fellow parishioners, and courage to be disliked by those who do not see our job as important.

Reflections

Introduction

The Vatican Council was not only a great theological redirecting of the Church, but also an ecclesial conversion in three major phases. In the years of the Council, the Church became aware of itself first of all as a community, then as a community living in the heart of the world, and finally as a community in the heart of the world in order to minister to the world. Community, incarnation, and ministry, then, are three conciliar insights that are universally applied to all the baptized. All Christians are life-giving members of this community; called to be sacrament of the world in the circumstances of their own lives, they are challenged to mission and ministry as a necessary part of their baptismal commitment.

Approaches to mission and ministry are the clearest indication of a generation's ecclesiology, and postconciliar efforts in this sphere are certainly indicative of a striving towards a new image of the Church. While this increase in the Church's self-understanding is being achieved with considerable pain and frustration, it is also a significant sign of hope and fidelity.

Renewal through Ministry

In the last twenty years, we have seen extraordinary developments in the Church's renewal through ministry. We have seen growth in a sense of service for all the baptized, we have rejoiced in the volunteer ministry of many, and above all we have welcomed the full-time professional commitment of increasing numbers of the faithful.

Full-time professional lay men and women received support in their commitment from John Paul II, who also warned of future difficulties in the area of role clarification. The U.S. bishops also welcomed this development of full-time ministry on the part of all the baptised, but they insisted: "All such ministries must be recognized by the community and authenticated by it in the person of its leader." Unfortunately, this has often resulted in a thwarting of baptismal equality and the growth of an employer-employee relationship in which the former not only hires, but also claims special divine guidance and sacramental grace to teach, govern, and sanctify. Full-time lay ecclesial ministers, like the priests, have given years of their life to training, but unlike the priests have had to finance it themselves. After ordination, the priest gets automatic placement irrespective of competence; the lay minister often lacks placement even though very well qualified. We need more time to clarify the process of authentication of lay ministry, and we would do well to parallel it with a process of ongoing evaluation of the pastoral performance of our bishops, priests, and deacons, so that the laity's authentication of clerics can be verified or not.

The integration of all the baptized into the mission of the Church is under way with powerful support from all areas of the Church. Ecclesial leaders are committed to facilitating ministry in laity. This is unquestionably one of the great signs of life in the Church of our times. There have been and still are problems, but determination to grow through them is also evident. The variety of ministries established by the Lord must be preserved or reintroduced where they have fallen into disuse. Laity cannot be deprived of those ministries that are a necessary fulfillment of their baptismal responsibilities. In this generation, part of the call of priests and religious is to facilitate the development of lay ministry and shared ministry. In fact, all approaches to the Church are partial without a shared responsibility in ministry. Such shared responsibility requires that each baptized Christian be guaranteed not only freedom in their responsible involvement in ministry, but also freedom of speech regarding what is seen to be best for the Church. This collaboration demands common vision, humility, and confidence in the Lord's support of all.

Since the Council, we have seen exceptional efforts in shared responsibility in the mission of the Church. Vision, guidance and challenge have come from many directions, and new areas of shared responsibility have developed. We have witnessed the growth of specialization in ministry, mobile interparish ministry, team ministry, and intervocational ministry. Dioceses and parishes have been restructured to foster and manifest shared responsibility, and Christians have been drawn into volunteering in ministries such as education, social services, and community building. Others felt free to explore new and creative approaches to ministry, and in many cases they have been welcomed and supported in their discoveries.

Shared responsibility is especially difficult where one person—willingly or unwillingly—represents the "establishment" and another stands for the "new breed." We still have far too much emphasis on ecclesiastical jurisdiction and insufficient consideration of charisms, and where this misplaced emphasis is verified, we have a theory of shared responsibility, but not the practice of it. In such cases, we really do not have shared ministry, but rather a lay participation in the hierarchy's mission. Talk about lay ministry often presumes that it is the ordained minister who is sharing his responsibility with others. Even in shared ministry, the layperson becomes the object of a clerical apostolate, either sharing in the minister's tasks or being commissioned to work in spheres where the clergy, and later the religious, have not had success. In this approach, laity are reduced to being the extended arm of the hierarchy.

When shared responsibility is applied in areas where laity are hired full-time for Church needs, other problems arise. Laity are hired because of competence, but they have no real authority resulting from position. They are accountable to the pastor who, while possibly far less qualified than the lay minister, has veto power over the layperson. The laity's ministry is generally task-oriented with little involvement in pastoral planning or policy, which is frequently reserved to the clergy. Although hired for their competence, the laity's permanence in their jobs does not always depend on competence but sometimes on the whim of the pastor.

Since it is more important to be Church than do anything, it is crucial that we see the difficulties overcome and the growth potential of laity furthered. Otherwise the exodus of the best career lay ministries will continue, or the redirecting of their dedication to nonecclesiastically controlled ministries will increase.

Initial Problems and Tensions in Ministry

Pope John Paul II, in one of his addresses to lay Church workers, anticipated several problems of laity in ministry, but urged all lay ministers to persevere through the early period of painful growth. "Hold fast to this [commitment], even if further clarification of your calling's form will still require reflection. If you do not receive from everyone in the communities that acceptance and welcome which you have so far experienced and which you have hoped for, it seems important to me that you should go on intelligently in hard situations above all, and remind yourselves of the idealism of your beginnings and try to win over other collaborators and communities gradually. We all believe that one and the same Spirit, who guides the communities and hearts of men, has summoned your service in the church into life. You are called to entrust yourselves to this Spirit precisely when faced with trouble" (John Paul II, "Address to Lay Church Workers," *Origins* 10 (1980): 394).

The pope speaks of the need for further clarification of the professional minister's calling. This will take time, research, and collaboration. However, many Church leaders are already voicing concern over what they see as the limited focus of ministry. While we are seeing a growth in inner-Church lay involvement, the bishops feel that the absence of Catholic lay involvement in the working world is "the single biggest problem facing the U.S. Church." John L. May, then Bishop of Mobile, Alabama, went even further in his criticism of the misdirection of lay ministry claiming that in some areas, such as labor management, politics, and higher education, Catholic laity are now exerting less leadership than before the Council (See Arthur

Jones, "Bishops: Laity Invisible to the World," *National Catholic Reporter,* 30 March 1979, p. 12).

From the time of the Council, laity have been challenged to bring a Christian spirit to the environment in which they live, and many lay associations have successfully done this. The bishops' concern remains a serious issue to address since the Church is not a sacrament for itself but a sacrament for the world. Perhaps the Church could look into the possibility of giving concrete financial aid to support structures for ministries of social involvement.

As well as recognizing the need for clarifying the layperson's calling, the pope also refers to the need for acceptance of lay ministry. Many are slow to accept a lay leader, especially in spiritual areas. A leadership role of a cleric or religious is passed on automatically to the succeeding cleric or religious but not so to a layperson. Each one must prove himself or herself. Yet role modeling, not competence, is the main short-run criterion, and this has often led to mimicking of the ordained minister in an undoubtedly subconscious effort to attain job security.

Another problem facing lay ministry today is the lack of support structures. Religious have their communities; priests have the priests' senate and the presbyterate, but laity in many dioceses have no ministry structure to support, inspire, and challenge them. They can become frustrated, their work can become routine, their ministry can become a job. Often financing comes from parishes, not dioceses, and it is the former that controls the lay minister and lay ministry. Diocesan support structures are difficult to establish for specific functions when each lay minister's job description is parish based. In spite of the excellent leadership of several dioceses, many other dioceses often offer no diocesan image of the various lay ministries. Added to the lack of common job descriptions for the minister is the problem of finance. The budget cutbacks of recent years have led to the termination of excellent lay ministers. Commitment to developing support structures is all the more urgent in this atmosphere to strengthen lay ministers' dedication and to contribute to their ongoing education and formation. Such structures are necessary for recruitment, placement, and accreditation.

In addition, support structures would help ease the problem of work stress in ministry. Burnout in full-time lay ministers is now high, and the opting out of volunteer work is also a problem. Researchers speak about work addiction, indicating that some ministers now demonstrate towards their work the typical signs of an addiction. Other ministers find career stagnation stressful. The establishing of support structures for the ongoing development of prayer, theological training, and social awareness is crucial at this time.

A further problem area that needs attention is the employment practices in the Church. I have referred to the lack of job descriptions, or worse still, the multiplicity of job descriptions, within the same local church. Many laity rightly see their work in education and social service as ministry but feel they are inexpensive labor for the Church. In most publicized cases throughout the nation, they have been denied the basic right to organize and bargain collectively. Admittedly, this should not be necessary, but unfortunately it often is. The teachings of the universal Church and the U.S. bishops are very clear on this point, but are frequently not practiced by dioceses in the U.S.

Salaries are low and place many full-time lay ministers with family responsibilities below the U.S. poverty level. Even so, they are frequently under the threat of competition from the even cheaper labor force of religious. If job security, fringe benefits, and good salary are the hope of anyone, then lay ministry is not the place to be. Even for those who are willing to work hard, live simply, and rely on the providence of the Lord for their future, the advancement opportunities in the Church are practically nonexistent. In spite of these many conflicts and problems, the whole development of lay ministry still heralds growth. Although the issue of lay ministry seems to be provoking an identity crisis for the Church-in-mission, in reality it offers an honest solution to the internal problems of the Church.

Tensions Resulting from the Different Understandings of Ministry Held by the Minister and the Community

A minister frequently finds that he or she has a different approach to the Church than the majority of the community. When the differences become extreme, the minister would do well to leave the local community, since the likelihood of achieving a common vision is very slight, and the price in stress will be high. Moreover, religious groups are no longer homogeneous in their profession of faith.

Rather, most members now identify only partially with a religious group's or Church's teachings. This is not bad; a healthy skepticism towards religion is contributing to a purifying of religious exaggerations and an overcoming of differences among the churches.

Most of the mainline Christian bodies now have two parallel churches within the local expressions of their faith. About two percent of each church is made up of professionals: clergy, laity, and religious. They are the "insiders" whose language, priorities, ethical systems, and interests show they are "churchy" people, part of the "official" Church. Others, the "outsiders," making up about 98 percent of each group, do not share the "insiders" vision of Church. Moreover, while being very dedicated, they neither understand the language and interests of the 2 percent, nor accept their priorities, vision, and ethical system. Several ministers will be among the 2 percent, and others among the 98 percent, provoking frustration in working with people of different ecclesiologies, those they serve, and those higher up in the structure.

A characteristic of religion, particularly in the United States, is that most churches now have a two-party system, with members who are conservative and others who are liberal. The stress caused by differences and polarization between members who claim the same faith but interpret it in different ways is especially painful to ministers who sense a calling to build up their communities.

Mainline churches that were formerly unified in living out their interpretation of Christianity are now divided into liberals, ultraliberals, middle of the road, conservatives, ultraconservatives. This structural diffusion of the churches forces the minister to live a chameleon model of ministry as he or she adapts as well as possible to the churches that now wear Joseph's coat of many colors.

The structural diffusion of the churches leads to the structural realignment of believers as liberals in one denomination feel more at home with liberals of another denomination than with conservatives of their own. Likewise conservatives of various traditions appreciate each other more than they do the liberals of their own group. This realignment of a community's members is again stressful to ministers whose relational skills are severely tested.

The internal divisions of the churches often leads to the developing of parallel ministries: a hierarchically controlled ministry and a freelance ministry. Some ministers who have worked for many years within church structures leave to set up a spontaneous form of the same ministry without it being ecclesiastically controlled. Thus many educators, social workers, family counselors, and others who see their work as ministry, leave church structures with their poor salaries, vetoes, caste system, secrecy, and inappropriate budget allocations to give themselves to the same essential ministry but without its secondary restrictive practices. This break is initially stressful, but the stress soon gives way to a peaceful expansion of Christian ministerial responsibility.

The sensitive minister trying to serve the people's religious needs finds that he or she must work skillfully with the psychological reactions of followers. People who are always liberal or always conservative in all they do are generally showing their basic psychological approach to life rather than any attitude of religious value. When openminded and openhearted Christians read scripture, they find it sometimes challenges them to live in a way that nonbelievers may judge to be conservative, and on other occasions it calls to attitudes that nonbelievers may well label liberal. People who are always conservative or always liberal generally read their own approach to life into scripture and out of it. They are not challenged by scripture but use it to express their psychological orientation to life.

The community and the minister often have a different understanding of ministry due to their different sociological approaches to life: some people value community, others independence; some are motivated by authority, others by influence; some are convinced their group's values work in practice, others have serious reservations; some emphasize the group's structured life, others their own spontaneity; some see obedience as leading to growth, others believe conflict and dissent are life-giving. If a minister has a different set of values than the community, or identifies several sociological approaches within the group, this is an added pressure on ministry.

Forces against Effective Leadership in Ministry

Many tensions in ministry result from an inadequate clarification of the minister's work. As already indicated, over 59 percent of all people who work for the churches have no job description, a situation that leads to additional conflict at the time of annual evaluation. Ministers without job descriptions tend to accumulate tasks depending on what other ministers do in neighborhood churches. This role accumulation sometimes means ministers are compared to other ministers whose responsibilities and salary may be considerably different than their own. As I have previously mentioned, I am not in favor of multiple job descriptions for a specific ministry within a local diocesan church since the practice leads to unjust comparisons and pressures. Moreover, when clear job descriptions are unavailable but responsibilities accumulate, a minister may find he or she becomes responsible for incompatible goals, such as being responsible for fostering a new image of Church among parishioners while maintaining income from bingo; or proclaiming the Church's teaching on justice while working in an unjust structure. A further stressful situation resulting from lack of clarity regarding the minister's work is misdirection of talents—when a skilled youth minister must give adult education programs, or a religious education minister finds himself or herself working with hurting families.

Some stressful situations develop because of the demands of the ministry. Some parishes or parish councils have unjustified expectations from lay pastoral ministers. The minister's responsibilities are many. They work long hours, sometimes fall prey to a work ethic adapted to ministry, and can end up overwhelmed by their work. As pressures of the ministry increase and demands of people multiply, a minister can fall into a situational depression that has the same characteristics as chronic depression but is not. Rather the depression results from the burdensome situation in which a minister works and will last as long, and only as long, as the burdensome situation does. If this situation is not remedied, then the minister moves towards burnout, a terrible experience that affects the most dedicated and eventually leads to hatred for the ministry that causes the oppressive burnout.

Some ministers, including pastors who are not priests, suffer from the underchallenge of ministry that can also lead to the serious symptoms of burnout. Dynamic visionaries get disheartened, working for a visionless church manager who has them involved in petty little projects to satisfy some parishioners' need for religious comfort. It is as discouraging to lay ministers as it used to be for the dedicated associate pastor kept in his place by an old-school pastor who may have had no intention of introducing the changes of Vatican II into the parish. Pressures of underchallenge are particularly acute for laity who know they have been excluded from major positions of ministry by the structure and laws. The minister can be further discouraged knowing the institution gained its authority over the course of two thousand years and is now dedicated more to self-preservation than it is to its original mission of outreach. Thus, many laity are reduced to being project directors, but their baptismal dignity and ministerial vocation require more than this.

Stressful situations in ministry sometimes provoke negative attitudes in the minister. If responsibilities are less than one's personal sense of vocation, the layperson can fall victim to a lack of self-esteem. Where pressures result from an oppressive working situation, the minister can find himself or herself frequently responding emotionally to issues. When one's ministry is not given adequate support, a layperson eventually lacks the resiliency to fight for the issue or to try again. Sometime the negative attitudes developed by laity portray a similar image to the negative dimensions of clericalism. This reaction gives the impression that these lay ministers think they are the new office holders of the Church, the new insiders. Ecclesiastical careerism is often associated with lay staffism. Career lay ministers need to constantly remind themselves that their long-term leadership depends on their ability to remain close to the people they serve. They must maintain their lay identity and refuse to see themselves as set apart from other laity. Some formation groups run the risks of setting the laity apart as a distinct rung on the institutional ladder. Some then subconsciously develop an image of themselves not unlike that associated with former clericalism.

Another force against effective leadership in lay ministry is the lack of the necessary skills. Every level of leadership requires both vision and skills, and if the latter are lacking, frustration results and the level of leadership usually fails. Ministry generally includes a dimension of management. Many programs for ministry training include such essential skills as budgeting, marketing, computer utilization, and human resource management. Unfortunately not all programs do, and it is annoying to see a good visionary and dedicated minister fail because he or she never acquired the requisite bureaucratic and management skills. In addition to these skills, ministers benefit from interpersonal skills of group development. When they are unaware of the stages of personal and group development, ministers lack the ability to use the processes necessary to achieve goals. Part of group development includes tension, ambiguity, criticism, and negativity—all components of a community's life with which ministers deal. Misuse and misunderstanding of conflict lead to many painful times for unskilled ministers. Likewise, theological vision and generous dedication bear little fruit without the skill to motivate those people ministers serve. Lack of appropriate skills after years of training is as disappointing and worrisome in lay ministers as it is in clergy.

Working in oppressive structures is a particularly stressful experience. Authoritarianism breeds oppression and dependency—all three non-Christian attitudes. An autocrat is an oppressed person who responds immaturely to the pressures of his or her environment. Such a nonleader is committed to the preservation of the oppressive structures that keep him or her in power. It is disconcerting to think that the many autocratic church managers we have known or worked under themselves feel oppressed and respond immaturely to the environmental pressures they encounter in their own ministry. Ministers who work with autocratic managers suffer from the oppressive authoritarianism and their own inability to change the structures that support it. The helplessness felt when one lacks resources to change oppressive structures can lead to a paralysis because of seemingly insurmountable problems.

There are several tensions that a minister meets precisely because he or she is working in religion. Religious leaders with a narrow view of Church and a weak commitment to community growth tend to build their own private kingdoms in which they govern with paternalism or maternalism. Often they are overinvolved in accumulating money to maintain the outward signs of power in church buildings, schools, clubs, and other parish facilities. Such religious managers fail to keep themselves upto date theologically and ministerially, often tending to become conservative stewards of the past. Other managers do not build an empire of church facilities and increased income, but their building consists in drawing people into their way of understanding ethics or religion. This ethical and religious colonialism is often linked to fundamentalism toward scripture in non-Catholics and toward official interpretations of Church teachings in Catholics. Ministers who know they are supported by ecclesiastical institutions get discouraged in working within them but often cannot leave, a situation that leads to further frustration.

Surviving Tensions in Ministry

Ministers who must live with the tensions of ministry need a healthy self-concept, must maintain a high degree of self-confidence and self-esteem, and need to be proud of their own talents and ministry. They need strong convictions, integrity, and the witness of their own Christian dedication. Today's ministers live with conflict and rejection, with frustration at their own ignorance regarding so many features of the Church's history and life, with pettiness internal to their own teams. Because their roles are new, they are judged more critically than priestly ministers used to be. In all this, laity need to be peaceful and confident in the quality of their own service and vision. Ministry is less what you do and more who you are, and all the pressures can be integrated into a healthy self-dedication to share in the servanthood of Jesus. Parishioners' criticisms often reflect an inability to accept change; low salary is not necessarily a personal evaluation of the minister, and budget cutbacks in a minister's programs do not always mean less appreciation of the individual. A woman minister's positive self-concept is threatened forcefully in an exclusively male Church that seems only to value masculine approaches to life. A result of this unhealthy approach is that some women, wishing to succeed, take on masculine attitudes that intensifies our problems. Rather, lay ministers must take pride in who they are, know their strengths as well as limitations, avoid seeing as a personal affront reactions that seem to be systemic for the Church. The minister needs to be characterized by optimism, enthusiasm, and joy in service.

Many problems in the post–Vatican II situation endure today. Many solutions have been tried and retried, and with much good will we still seem blocked in our overriding desire to find some way out of our problems. Ministry always requires some trial and error and acceptance of colleagues' different views and divided loyalties. But ministers today also need the prophetic quality of creativity so they can discover alternative solutions to perennial problems. A minister exercises creativity first towards himself or herself in discovering ways to integrate leisure into life, to foster spiritual growth when no models exist for the contemporary minister, to build a schedule that allows distance from work and adequate quality time for friends and family. We search for new ends not new means. The vision for this comes out of contemplation, study, sharing, and extensive reading, and it builds on the natural qualities of intelligence and imagination. Genuine love and dedication to those we serve show themselves in ongoing preparation and self-enrichment for the ministerial tasks we carry out for others.

I have already mentioned the importance of strong support systems for the contemporary minister who works within Church structures. Without the support of prayer, study, and sharing—of peer support, team support, and management support; of deep friendship for the unmarried and satisfying sexual relations for the married such that both will lead to the supports of intimacy—it is difficult to maintain strong and effective commitment to ministry. These support systems are not built up without considerable effort and practical rearrangement of one's priorities, especially in the use of time. Ministers and those who hire them are becoming acutely aware of the importance of support systems for both enrichment and maintenance. Without the updating, friendship, shared experience, and healthy adult give and take that support systems provide the minister's leadership effectiveness will be seriously jeopardized. Nevertheless, building support systems is frequently neglected by professional lay ministers. Those who think they can go it alone often end in burnout. Those who rely exclusively on their spouse often end sharing the frustration and potential burnout with the one they love most. The universal Church's experience of the effects of lonely ministry shows that it frequently leads to maladjusted personalities, alcoholism, and worse. This should challenge us all to insist on support structures for ourselves and for those ministers for whom we may have responsibility.

Job effectiveness is itself a major support to ministers, bringing them peace, satisfaction, acceptance, and positive appreciation. Ministers now give thought to the specific supports of pastoral ministry. These include their initial training, ongoing education, appropriate skills workshops, ability to work with groups, aptitudes to preside. Few dimensions of ministry are as supportive as success. However, in ministry the challenge is increasingly who we become as a result of our Christian service to others. Consequently, a major support that aids in a satisfying and effective approach to our work is establishing a solid spirituality. Growth in discipleship does not take place in our spare time but only through quality life in the major moments of each day. This spirituality is not something that we bring to ministry, but something that our specific ministries determine. The innumerable forms of spirituality for the various conditions of lay ministry necessarily come out of lay experience. At present, the universal official Church has little to offer in this undertaking, but lay ministers foster a new spirituality by being creative in their ideas, honest in what is spiritually life-giving, and willing to act as mentors or even spiritual guides for other less experienced lay ministers. While the components of lay spirituality will differ, ten characteristics form a possible common core:

1. An awareness of baptismal vocation
2. A realization that life is grace and gift
3. Conscience formation
4. Dedication to the local church
5. Work
6. Building community at all levels
7. Integration of the joys of life
8. Prayer growth
9. Service
10. Prophetic outreach. (See Leonard Doohan, "Lay Spirituality for the Future," *Praying,* January/February 1988, 12–14, 30).

A Concluding Reflection on Tensions in Ministry

When Matthew's Gospel gave us the mission discourse in chapter ten, he found his source material in Mark's Gospel, chapter thirteen. The latter spoke of the pains and anguish that would precede the end of the world. Matthew, ministering to a church that was struggling to understand itself in a changing world, found that ministry had already become a painful form of dedication to the Lord and his people. What Mark thought would only happen at the end of the world, Matthew already sees as the trials his ministers face. Mark wrote his Gospel for a suffering church and stressed the need that disciples awaken from their sleep to the reality that they too are in the garden of Gethsemane. He even challenges them to remove their willful blindness and to see that they follow the suffering Jesus.

I meet many laity who always wanted to be involved ministerially in the life of the Church and who enter enthusiastically into the new opportunities. Sometimes individuals who have been hurt, abused, separated, or divorced, also enter the service of a loving Church. But the Church, with all its love, hope, and mutual service, can easily become for the minister a place of hurt and abuse, with little support and little love. Today's ministers must be willing to be unloved.

A decision to be involved in ministry is not easily made. Many pray, discern, go on retreats, and need much encouragement to accept the call. Once a decision is made, we mutually encourage each other to persevere in ministry, not in spite of problems or with resignation to the difficulties we meet, but rather with the kind of peace and Christian sensitivity that indicates we expected suffering. While situations of difficulty, hurt, and oppression must be challenged to change, some lay ministers' criticism seems to indicate they did not expect the problems or do not see them as integral to their call. We all need to be mature enough to live out the implications of our response to the Lord's call to ministry.

Many of the stressful situations referred to in this chapter have emerged with the development of lay ministry. Some would like them to be resolved as quickly as possible. I also think it is necessary to savor this pain and grieve over the differences we experience. To savor the pain may help us to cherish the values we seek and the successes we may gain. This is as true in our local teams as it is in encounters with official Church management. Laity bring considerable skill to this venture, since they have long learned to grieve over the pains of family separation, the differences between spouses, the rejection by children, and painful conflicts at work. Grief helps us to let go of the past, realize how precious are the changes we seek, and truly be compassionate. This grieving does not exclude constant struggling against injustice, nor does it encourage a passivity that easily leads to burnout. It reminds us that the mystery of the cross is as intimately linked to ministry as is the joy of the resurrection.

Jesus showed some reluctance to accept the pain and suffering of his ministry and even prayed that the chalice might pass. That episode shows how difficult it is to accept the painful consequences of ministry. But after a moment's hesitation, Jesus rededicates himself to the only form ministry can take. As disbelievers in Mark's Gospel echo the appeal, "Come down from the cross and we will believe" (Mark 15:27–32), believers know that that is precisely what Jesus cannot do if he is to be true to his call. Contemporary leaders can do no differently. The tensions of leadership are integral to ministry. When present ones are worked through, others will arise. These stressful situations, even crises, are opportunities for the minister to identify with the servant Christ.

Critical Issues and Tensions in Ministry

Conflict Management

Christianity in general and Catholicism in particular cannot be portrayed as monolithic unified groups with a common image. Constructive conflict, a sign of organizational vitality, will increasingly characterize religion, Christianity, and Catholicism. In fact, it is difficult to envisage the absence of strategic conflict between groups within a church or members of a team. Not all conflict leads to growth, some friction festers and degenerates into unresolved anger.

How do you act in times of conflict? Can you identify major causes of conflict for you? Is it people, situations, attitudes, or topics that lead to conflict? Do you deal with the specific issue or do you personalize it? Thomas Sweetser and Carol Wisniewski Holden (*Leadership in a Successful Parish* 97–104) speak of five styles of managing conflict: (1) In the Win/Lose Style, a minister achieves his or her goal but damages relationships in the process. (2) The Accommodating Style refers to a conflict situation in which a minister preserves the relationship with others at the price of not achieving the goal. (3) The Avoidance Style describes a reaction to conflict used by pessimistic individuals to escape conflict by "turning off" or leaving the team discussion. (4) The Compromise Style manifests itself when both sides yield a little, no one is fully satisfied, but conflict is avoided. (5) The Win/Win Style is the desirable reaction and is present when each one goes all out to achieve his or her goal but treats others' opinions as seriously as one's own. The appropriate strategy to manage conflict focuses on the person whose emotional reaction identifies him or her as the one with the conflict.

The following are qualities identifiable in healthy conflict management: There is a good relationship between the parties, each accepting conflict as a part of growth. Each person involved in the situation of conflict is willing to be involved with others in any attempts to resolve the crisis and is ready to change. Each of the persons in conflict must deal with real facts and never another's motives. And finally, the issue is dealt with briefly, resolved, and both sides move on, forgetting the past, accepting the consequences of conflict, and bearing no grudges.

Conflict is a constant component of church life. Ministers can receive benefits from reflecting on the situations of conflict within the early Church. Identify the skills and attitudes shown between church ministers in the following episodes:

Acts 6:1–6	The Eleven and the Hellenists
Acts 11:1–18	Peter and the Elders
Acts 15:1–12	Members of the Council of Jerusalem
Gal. 2:11–14	Paul and Peter
Acts 15:36–40	Paul and Barnabas
Acts 21:17–26	Paul and the Jerusalem authorities
2 Cor. 1:12–2:11	Paul and the Corinthians
Gal. 1:6–10	Paul and the Galatians
Philemon	Paul and Philemon

Burnout in Ministry

Burnout is a growing problem for career lay ministers. Excessive stress affects the most dedicated of the Church's ministers. This alarming problem challenges professionals to develop new skills to identify symptoms and prevent crisis.

Areas of Stress in Ministry.

The profound and rapid changes of modern life challenge us to constantly change and be creative in responding to the complexities of life. For people in ministry the changes in the direction of the Church challenge them. Sometimes other people's unwillingness to change is also stressful for the minister. At times it is necessary to work with people who have different value systems than one's own, and as a result, many arrive at group decisions with considerable pain. Where differences are notable, an absence of the basic affirmation in work that we all need results. With the increased pressures of ministry, some individuals set unrealistic goals for themselves and are unable to say "no" to each day's many needs. This "savior" mentality produces an inability to separate devotion to work from personal life. These sociological and ministerial challenges are often intensified by the constant need to meet deadlines and the financial pressures due to poor salaries. Personal areas of stress include a perfectionist tendency that, when unmet, leads to a constant lack of self-esteem. Changes in the Church produce either a resistance to the change or anger at the lack of it. Recent forms of collaborative ministry, with their demands for new skills, also lead to stress when ministers are unable to work with groups.

Development of Burnout

When the stresses of life become so great that we can no longer cope with them, they lead to distress. When the stresses result from the pressures of interactions with people, they lead to the possible development of burnout. This phenomenon does not necessarily result from overwork. In fact, the workaholic is not a candidate for burnout, since he or she uses work as an escape from people. It is when people in the helping professions, like ministers, make other people and their crises part of their own life that burnout begins. It develops in three stages. First, ministers become dissatisfied at work, feel a lack of appreciation from others, and begin to isolate themselves. This stage does not affect the quality of work and is not easily noticed since its symptoms are the same as other stressful situations. Second, a time of self-questioning leads to a feeling of helplessness and frustration. This becomes so great that job performance begins to suffer. Third, terminal burnout is present when individuals begin to mechanically perform their tasks without any real interest or involvement. They feel intense loneliness, become sour on life, and often manifest an open rebellion that completely disrupts their work. The last stage ends with individuals hating the very situation that they believe causes their stress, which for ministers is the very vocational commitment about which at one time they were so enthusiastic.

The symptoms of burnout are similar to those of general stress: headaches, insomnia, loss of appetite, irritability, fatigue, chest pains, and lack of energy. One loses the desire to go to one's place of work and is unable to associate with others. The potential burnout victim becomes constantly discouraged, angry, or overly sensitive to casual remarks. The absence of peace, together with an inability to pray and a loss of enthusiasm, leads to a sense of hopelessness.

Prevention of Burnout.

The early stages of burnout are not easily identifiable, and when one begins to experience burnout, the natural reaction is to intensify work to prove to oneself and others that there is really no problem. Once the cycle begins, it is very difficult to arrest it. Hence, prevention is critical. Here are some practical suggestions to insure a lifestyle that avoids burnout.

1. Admit the seriousness of stress in ministry.
2. Give adequate time to prayer, work, friendship, and leisure, thus developing broad interests.
3. Provide for suitable education and theological updating.
4. Appreciate the depth and limits of one's vocation as a call to "be" not to "do."
5. Insure adequate human resource management, including support, encouragement, and feedback.
6. Improve the quality of the working environment.
7. Develop a healthy self-concept and justified self-esteem.
8. Establish appropriate support structures.
9. Redefine success in ministry so as to benefit from job satisfaction.
10. Foster a mutually supportive working environment.
11. Maintain deep relationships.
12. Care for yourself physically with proper nutrition, regular exercise, and sufficient sleep.

A Self-Test for Satisfaction in One's Work

	Agree				Disagree
	5	4	3	2	1
1. Do you like the environment you work in?					
2. Do you enjoy working with the people in your office?					
3. Do you have sufficient autonomy to do your work?					
4. Are you treated with respect by members of your team?					
5. Do you maintain distance between your working life and your private time?					

	Agree				Disagree
	5	4	3	2	1

6. Do you have the skills you think you need for your ministry?
7. Does the local church give you adequate budget support for your area of responsibility?
8. Can you motivate others?
9. Are you free from major job-related anxieties?
10. Do you feel stimulated and excited about your work?
11. Does your work give you hope?
12. Are you given adequate information regarding your areas of responsibility?

Your score should be 50 or over to indicate job satisfaction.

Topics for Reflection and Discussion

A Personal Review of One's Ministry: Questions for Personal Meditation

1. How have you struggled for acceptance as a "nonpriest" in your pastoral ministry?
2. What are the experiences of loneliness that your present ministry brings?
3. What forms of institutionalized sin have you met in your ministry?
4. Do you feel you are an insider or an outsider to Church ministry? Why?
5. What are the major rewards of your ministry?
6. Think of a situation in ministry when you were convinced the Lord was working through you. What qualities were highlighted?
7. Recall the history of your own call to ministry.
8. Are you content and at peace with yourself in your ministry?
9. What is the relationship of your spirituality to your ministry?

Questions for Group Sharing

1. What can laity teach priests and religious regarding spiritual growth?

2. How does the prayer of laity differ from that of religious or priests?
3. Is sexual love a help or hindrance to Christian growth?
4. In what ways can laity live out the cross of Christ and share in his passion?
5. How have laity replaced in their own lives the decrease in practices and devotions offered by the local parish?
6. How have the spiritual movements helped lay life? Have they hindered it?
7. What do laity need to do now to be ready for the rapidly changing world of tomorrow?
8. Why is social involvement a necessary part of Christian spirituality?
9. How is the universal Church benefiting from the increased dedication of laity?
10. Who are the outstanding laity in your life? What do you admire about them?

Some Concerns of Lay Ministers about Tensions in Ministry

One tension is dealing with a husband who deeply resents time spent away from him, time given to the Church. He is proud of my ministry, but traditional and uncomfortable with his inability to control.

•

Learning to say "no" brings a lot of stress. There's no end to what can be done. Learning to put an end to what will be done is stressful. My position attracts a lot of comments and criticisms from many different people—another source of tension and stress.

•

There's always more to do. Tensions do not always fall into predominantly task orientations, but it is even stressful to maintain prayerfulness, to be discerning about what to say "yes" to, to resist being controlled by anxieties, perfectionism, others' unrealistic demands and expectations.

•

At times the people in the parish think I only work on Sundays, and say a wealthy church is wasting its money on these jobs. Organizing activities that are considered "unsuccessful" is also stressful.

•

In our staff the tensions were (1) being a woman, and (2) working with immature or power-hungry clergy.

Selected Reading

Bausch William. *Traditions, Tensions, Transitions in Ministry.* Mystic, CT: Twenty-Third Publications, 1982.

Doohan, Helen. *The Minister of God: Effective and Fulfilled.* Staten Island, NY: Alba House, 1986.

Flagel, Clarice. *Avoiding Burnout: Time Management for DREs.* Dubuque, IA: William C. Brown, 1981.

Lewis, A. Douglass. *Resolving Church Conflicts.* San Francisco: Harper & Row, 1981.

Weidman, Judith L., ed. *Women Ministers: How Women Are Redefining Traditional Roles.* San Francisco: Harper & Row, 1981.

Additional Reading

Doohan, Leonard. *The Laity: A Bibliography.* Wilmington, DE: Michael Glazier, Inc., 1987. See sections 23, 30.

SCRIPTURE READINGS FOR PERSONAL OR GROUP REFLECTION ON MINISTRY

These Scripture readings are given for prayerful reflection. They deal with Jesus as a model for ministers today, fruitfulness in ministry, and the call and challenge that lie before each dedicated minister. They also focus on the call to spiritual growth and the staff's communal challenge in their life together. Finally, those references are given that remind contemporary ministers of the attitudes Jesus required in those who wished to minister in his name.

Jesus as a Model for Ministers

"At the sight of the crowds, his heart was moved with pity." (Matt. 9:36)

"Did you not know that I must be in my Father's house?" (Luke 2:49)

"The Spirit of the Lord is upon me,
because he has anointed me
    to bring glad tidings to the poor.
He has sent me to proclaim liberty to captives
    and recovery of sight to the blind,
        to let the oppressed go free,
and to proclaim a year acceptable to the Lord." (Luke 4:18–19)

"I have come to set the earth on fire, and how I wish it were already blazing!" (Luke 12:49)

"I tell you, in just the same way there will be more joy in heaven over one sinner who repents than over ninety-nine righteous people who have no need of repentance." (Luke 15:7)

"I am among you as the one who serves." (Luke 22:27)

"For God did not send his Son into the world to condemn the world, but that the world might be saved through him." (John 3:17)

"I am the good shepherd, and I know mine and mine know me." (John 10:14)

"I have other sheep that do not belong to this fold. These also I must lead, and they will hear my voice, and there will be one flock, one shepherd." (John 10:16)

"As you have sent me into the world, so I sent them into the world. And I consecrate myself for them, so that they also may be consecrated in truth." (John 17:18–19)

"This is my commandment: love one another as I love you." (John 15:12)

"Remember the word I spoke to you, 'No slave is greater than his master.' If they persecuted me, they will also persecute you. If they kept my word, they will also keep yours." (John 15:20)

"I pray not only for them, but also for those who will believe in me through their word, so that they may all be one, as you, Father, are in me and I in you, that they also may be in us, that the world may believe that you sent me." (John 17:20–21)

Fruitfulness in Ministry

"Ask and it will be given to you; seek and you will find; knock and the door will be opened to you." (Matt. 7:7)

"Whoever receives you receives me, and whoever receives me receives the one who sent me." (Matt. 10:40)

"I say to you, if you have faith the size of a mustard seed, you will say to this mountain, 'Move from here to there,' and it will move. Nothing will be impossible for you." (Matt. 17:20)

"This is how it is with the kingdom of God; it is as if a man were to scatter seed on the land and would sleep and rise night and day and the seed would sprout and grow, he knows not how." (Mark. 4:26–27)

"Whoever listens to you listens to me. Whoever rejects you rejects me. And whoever rejects me rejects the one who sent me." (Luke 10:16)

"Let anyone who thirsts come to me and drink. Whoever believes in me, as scripture says:

'Rivers of living water will flow from within him.' " (John 7:37–38)

"I say to you, Whoever believes in me will do the works I do, and will do greater ones than these." (John 14:12)

"If you ask anything of me in my name, I will do it." (John 14:14)

"I am the vine, you are the branches. Whoever remains in me and I in him will bear much fruit, because without me you can nothing." (John 15:5)

"Now to him who is able to accomplish far more than all we ask or imagine, by the power at work within us, to him be glory in the church and in Christ Jesus to all generations, forever and ever. Amen." (Eph. 3:20–21)

The Minister's Call and Challenge

"Everyone who acknowledges me before others I will acknowledge before my heavenly Father." (Matt. 10:32)

"I say to you, many prophets and righteous people longed to see what you see but did not see it, and to hear what you hear but did not hear it." (Matt. 13:17)

"Jesus said to his disciples, 'Whoever wishes to come after me must deny himself, take up his cross, and follow me. For whoever wishes to save his life will lose it, but whoever loses his life for my sake will find it.' " (Matt. 16:24–25)

"Go, therefore, and make disciples of all the nations, baptizing them in the name of the Father, and of the Son, and of the holy Spirit." (Matt. 28:19)

"Come after me, I will make you fishers of men." (Mark 1:17)

"Go, sell what you have, and give to [the] poor and you will have treasure in heaven; then come, follow me." (Mark 10:21)

"And you, child, will be called prophet of the Most High,
    for you will go before the Lord to prepare his ways." (Luke 1:76)

"He said to him, 'Follow me.' And leaving everything behind, he got up and followed him." (Luke 5:27–28)

"Everyone of you who does not renounce all his possessions cannot be my disciple." (Luke 14:33)

"From his fullness we have all received, grace in place of grace." (John 1:16)

"I say to you, no one can enter the kingdom of God without being born of water and Spirit." (John 3:5)

"I am the light of the world. Whoever follows me will not walk in darkness, but will have the light of life." (John 8:12)

"If you remain in my word, you will truly be my disciples, and you will know the truth, and the truth will set you free." (John 8:31–32)

"Whoever serves me must follow me, and where I am, there also will my servant be. The Father will honor whoever serves me." (John 12:26)

"Whoever loves me will keep my word." (John 14:23)

"As the Father loves me, so I also love you. Remain in my love." (John 15:9)

"It was not you who chose me, but I who chose you and appointed you to go and bear fruit." (John 15:16)

"And you also testify, because you have been with me from the beginning." (John 15:27)

"Because the words you gave to me I have given to them, and they accepted them and truly understood that I came from you, and they have believed that you sent me." (John 17:8)

"Keep watch over yourselves and over the whole flock of which the holy Spirit has appointed you overseers, in which you tend the church of God that he acquired with his own blood." (Acts 20:28)

"Proclaim the word; be persistent whether it is convenient or inconvenient; convince, reprimand, encourage through all patience and teaching." (2 Tim. 4:2)

"Grace and peace from God the Father and Christ Jesus our savior." (Titus 1:4)

"But you are 'a chosen race, a royal priesthood, a holy nation, a people of his own, so that you may announce the praises' of him who called you out of darkness into his wonderful light." (1 Pet. 2:9)

"Tend the flock of God in your midst, [overseeing] not by constraint but willingly, as God would have it, not for shameful profit but eagerly." (1 Pet. 5:2)

The Minister's Personal Spiritual Life

"[But] take care not to perform religious deeds in order that people may see them." (Matt. 6:1)

"O you of little faith? . . . do not worry." (Matt. 6:30–31)

"Everyone who listens to these words of mine and acts on them will be like a wise man who built his house on rock." (Matt. 7:24)

"No disciple is above his teacher, no slave above his master. It is enough for the disciple that he become like his teacher, for the slave that he become like his master." (Matt. 10:24–25)

"Come to me, all you who labor and are burdened, and I will give you rest. Take my yoke upon you and learn from me, for I am meek and humble of heart; and you will find rest for yourselves. For my yoke is easy, and my burden light." (Matt. 11:28–30)

"I say to you, unless you turn and become like children, you will not enter the kingdom of heaven. Whoever humbles himself like this child is the greatest in the kingdom of heaven." (Matt. 18:3–4)

"This is the time of fulfillment. The kingdom of God is at hand. Repent, and believe in the gospel!" (Mark 1:15)

"A prophet is not without honor except in his native place and among his own kin and in his own house." (Mark 6:4)

"Can you drink the cup that I drink or be baptized with the bapitism with which I am baptized?" (Mark 10:38)

"Blessed are those who hear the word of God and observe it." (Luke 11:28)

"Much will be required of the person entrusted with much, and still more will be demanded of the person entrusted with more." (Luke 12:48)

"Pray that you may not undergo the test." (Luke 22:40)

"Whoever lives the truth comes to the light, so that his works may be clearly seen as done in God." (John 3:21)

"He must increase; I must decrease." (John 3:30)

"Whoever drinks the water I shall give will never thirst; the water I shall give will become in him a spring of water welling up to eternal life." (John 4:14)

"No one can come to me unless the Father who sent me draw him, and I will raise him on the last day. It is written in the prophets:
'They shall all be taught by God.'
Everyone who listens to my Father and learns from him comes to me." (John 6:44–45)

"I am the living bread that came down from heaven; whoever eats this bread will live forever; and the bread that I will give is my flesh for the life of the world." (John 6:51)

"Peace I leave with you; my peace I give to you. Not as the world gives do I give it to you. Do not let you hearts be troubled or afraid." (John 14:27)

"I am the true vine, and my Father is the vine grower. He takes away every branch in me that does not bear fruit, and everyone that does he prunes so that it bears more fruit." (John 15:1–2)

"Keep in mind the words of the Lord Jesus who himself said, 'It is more blessed to give than to receive.' " (Acts 20:35)

"Let no one deceive himself. If anyone among you considers himself wise in this age, let him become a fool so as to become wise. For the wisdom of this world is foolishness in the eyes of God. (1 Cor. 3:18–19)

If any of you lacks wisdom, he should ask God who gives to all generously and ungrudgingly, and he will be given it. (James 1:5)

The Team's/Staff's Life in Collaboration

"But I say to you, whoever is angry with his brother will be liable to judgment." (Matt. 5:22)

"Stop judging, that you may not be judged. For as you judge, so will you be judged, and the measure with which you measure will be measured out to you." (Matt. 7:1–2)

"Do to others whatever you would have them do to you. This is the law and the prophets." (Matt. 7:12)

"Woe to the world because of things that cause sin! Such things must come, but woe to the one through whom they come!" (Matt. 18:7)

"If your brother sins [against you], go and tell him his fault between you and him alone." (Matt. 18:15)

"Again, [amen,] I say to you, if two of you agree on earth about anything for which they are to pray, it shall be granted to them by my heavenly Father. For where two or three are gathered together in my name, there am I in the midst of them." (Matt. 18:19–20)

"Whoever wishes to be great among you shall be your servant; whoever wishes to be first among you shall be your slave." (Matt. 20:26–27)

For there is nothing hidden except to be made visible; nothing is secret except to come to light. (Mark 4:22)

"Come away by yourselves to a deserted place and rest a while." (Mark 6:31)

"Whatever you have said in the darkness will be heard in the light, and what you have whispered behind closed doors will be proclaimed on the housetops." (Luke 12:3)

"Do not be afraid any longer, little flock, for your Father is pleased to give you the kingdom." (Luke 12:32)

"If, therefore, you are not trustworthy with dishonest wealth, who will trust you with true wealth?" (Luke 16:11)

"Were not our hearts burning [within us] while he spoke to us on the way and opened the scriptures to us?" (Luke 24:32)

"He was made known to them in the breaking of bread." (Luke 24:35)

> "And we saw his glory,
> the glory as of the Father's only Son,
> full of grace and truth." (John 1:14)

"I tell you, look up and see the fields ripe for the harvest." (John 4:35)

"If I, therefore, the master and teacher, have washed your feet, you ought to wash one another's feet. I have given you a model to follow, so that as I have done for you, you should also do." (John 13:14–15)

"Love one another. As I have loved you, so you also should love one another. This is how all will know that you are my disciples, if you have love for one another." (John 13:34–35)

"Behold, the hour is coming and has arrived when each of you will be scattered to his own home and you will leave me alone." (John 16:32)

"I made known to them your name and I will make it known, that the love with which you loved me may be in them and I in them." (John 17:26)

"Love one another with mutual affection; anticipate one another in showing honor. Do not grow slack in zeal, be fervent in spirit, serve the Lord." (Rom. 12:10–11)

"I urge you . . . in the name of our Lord Jesus Christ, that all of you agree in what you say, and that there be no divisions among you, but that you be united in the same mind and in the same purpose." (1 Cor. 1:10)

"Thus should one regard us: as servants of Christ and stewards of the mysteries of God. Now it is of course required of stewards that they be found trustworthy." (1 Cor. 4:1–2)

"There are different kinds of spiritual gifts but the same Spirit; there are different forms of service but the same Lord; there are different workings but the same God who produces all of them in everyone. To each individual the manifestation of the Spirit is given for some benefit." (1 Cor. 12:4–7)

"If [one] part suffers, all the parts suffer with it; if one part is honored, all the parts share its joy." (1 Cor. 12:26)

"Love is patient, love is kind. It is not jealous, [love] is not pompous, it is not inflated, it is not rude, it does not seek its own interests, it is not quick-tempered, it does not brood over injury." (1 Cor. 13:4–5)

"Preserve the unity of the Spirit through the bond of peace." (Eph. 4:3)

"So let us confidently approach the throne of grace to receive mercy and to find grace for timely help." (Heb. 4:16)

"Finally, all of you, be of one mind, sympathetic, loving toward one another, compassionate, humble." (1 Pet. 3:8)

> "What we have seen and heard we proclaim now to you,
> so that you too may have fellowship with us;
> for our fellowship is with the Father
> and with his Son, Jesus Christ." (1 John 1:3)

"Let us love not in word or speech but in deed and truth." (1 John 3:18)

"Beloved, do not trust every spirit but test the spirits to see whether they belong to God." (1 John 4:1)

Attitudes in Ministry

"You are the light of the world. A city set on a mountain cannot be hidden. Nor do they light a lamp and then put it under a bushel basket; it is set on a lampstand, where it gives light to all in the house." (Matt. 5:14–15)

"You are the salt of the earth. But if salt loses its taste, with what can it be seasoned?" (Matt. 5:13)

"Beware of false prophets, who come to you in sheep's clothing, but underneath are ravenous wolves. By their fruits you will know them." (Matt. 7:15–16)

"Go and learn the meaning of the words, 'I desire mercy, not sacrifice.' " (Matt. 9:13)

"People do not put new wine into old wineskins. Otherwise the skins burst, the wine spills out, and the skins are ruined. Rather, they pour new wine into fresh wineskins, and both are preserved." (Matt. 9:17)

"Without cost you have received; without cost you are to give." (Matt. 10:8)

"Behold, I am sending you like sheep in the midst of wolves; so be shrewd as serpents and simple as doves." (Matt. 10:16)

"A good person brings forth good out of a store of goodness." (Matt. 12:35)

"Every scribe who has been instructed in the kingdom of heaven is like the head of a household who brings from his storeroom both the new and the old." (Matt. 13:52)

"See that you do not despise one of these little ones, for I say to you that their angels in heaven always look upon the face of my heavenly Father." (Matt. 18:10)

"If a man has a hundred sheep and one of them goes astray, will he not leave the ninety-nine in the hills and go in search of the stray?" (Matt. 18:12)

"I say to you, whatever you did for one of these least brothers of mine, you did for me." (Matt. 25:40)

"To the other towns also I must proclaim the good news of the kingdom of God, because for this purpose I have been sent." (Luke 4:43)

"Be merciful, just as [also] your Father is merciful. Stop judging and you will not be judged." (Luke 6:36–37)

"What is impossible for human beings is possible for God." (Luke 18:27)

"No one can receive anything except what has been given him from heaven." (John 3:27)

"Do not let your hearts be troubled. You have faith in God; have faith also in me." (John 14:1)

"Remain in me, as I remain in you. Just as a branch cannot bear fruit on its own unless it remains on the vine, so neither can you unless you remain in me." (John 15:4)

"I did not shrink from proclaiming to you the entire plan of God." (Acts 20:27)

"If anyone builds on this foundation with gold, silver, precious stones, wood, hay, or straw, the work of each will come to light, for the Day will disclose it. (1 Cor. 3:12–13)

"Persevere in prayer, being watchful in it with thanksgiving." (Col. 4:2)

"You must say what is consistent with sound doctrine." (Titus 2:1)

"Do not lord it over those assigned to you, but be examples to the flock." (1 Pet. 5:3)

Additional Reading

Doohan, Leonard. *Matthew: Spirituality for the '80s and '90s.* Santa Fe, NM: Bear and Co., 1985.

———. *Luke: The Perennial Spirituality.* 2d ed., Santa Fe, NM: Bear and Co., 1985.

———. *Mark: Visionary of Early Christianity.* Santa Fe, NM: Bear and Co., 1986.

———. *John: Gospel for a New Age.* Santa Fe, NM: Bear and Co., 1988.

Appendix 2:

PROFESSIONAL ORGANIZATIONS
FOR LAITY

International Liaison (Catholic Coordinating Center for Lay Volunteer Ministries)
  810 Rhode Island Avenue, N.E.,
  Washington, DC 20018

National Association for Lay Ministry
  Suite 2-67.
  1125 West Baseline Rd.
  Mesa, AZ 85202

National Association of Church Personnel Administrators,
  NACPA National Office,
  100 E. Eighth St.,
  Cincinnati, OH 45202

National Association of Parish Coordinators/Directors (NAPC/D),
  Suite 100, 1077 Thirtieth St, N.W.
  Washington, DC 20007

National Conference of Diocesan Directors,
  3021 Fourth St., N.E.
  Washington, DC 20017

National Federation for Catholic Youth Ministry,
  3900-A Harewood Rd., N.E.
  Washington, DC 20017

INDEX